A Radical Philosophy

A Radical Philosophy

AGNES HELLER

Translated by James Wickham

Basil Blackwell

English translation © Basil Blackwell Publisher Limited 1984
First published in German as *Philosophie des
linken Radikalismus* © Agnes Heller 1978
represented by Eulama Literary Agency

English translation first published 1984

Basil Blackwell Publisher Limited
108 Cowley Road, Oxford OX4 1JF, England

Basil Blackwell Inc.
432 Park Avenue South, Suite 1505
New York, NY 10016, USA

British Library Cataloguing in Publication Data
Heller, Agnes
  A radical philosophy.
  1. Philosophy, Marxist
  I. Title   II. Philosophie des Linken
  Radikalismus. *English*
  335.4'11   B809.8

ISBN 0–631–12567–1

Typeset by Oxford Publishing Services
Printed in Great Britain by Billings & Son Ltd, Worcester

Contents

1

Introduction: Waking from the Dogmatic Dream

Novalis' aphorism that philosophy has to explain not nature but philosophy itself put forward a programme for philosophy that no philosopher in the preceding twelve hundred years would have understood. Naturally, before the bourgeois revolutions the philosophers analysed the characteristics and the nature of their own work — Socrates, the first philosopher, had already done this. However, up until Novalis, self-reflection was for philosophy not its primary task and not even an urgent task. Self-reflection was always subordinated to what was the grand task, the real task — namely, the constitution of a world. It is no accident that philosophy's concern with *self-knowledge* and with self-reflection as its own unique task appears at the same time as Schiller's commitment to *sentimental art*. Philosophy and art both questioned the same thing — naivety. In the same way as art can no longer "sing as the birds sing", so philosophy has to wake from its "dogmatic dream".

It would take us too far to attempt to write the "parallel biographies" of art and philosophy since the period of the bourgeois revolutions. However, the parallels must be indicated so that it is possible to understand how the legitimation crisis of modern philosophy cannot be deduced from the expansion of the "sciences". It is not the advance of the sciences which has made philosophy "rootless", even though it always has to give way to them with an ever worse conscience — just as since Bacon and Descartes (and with an equally bad conscience) religion has had to give way to philosophy.

Philosophy began to present itself in the garb of the "exact sciences", it began to attempt to confirm itself before them, claiming to be not *just as* "exact" as them, but *exactly* as "exact" as them. It is not as if philosophy had not always aspired to *scientificity*; it did so, but it used different standards. We can say, with Hume, that it has created its own standards from its own sovereignty. It is hardly surprising that its guilty retreat in front of science produced a counter-tendency. This however involved another surrender: philosophy gave ground to *religion*, which in the century of the Enlightenment it had already once defeated. The religion that is involved here is no longer any positive religion, but only a religious *attitude*, the preference for belief instead of knowledge — something that rests on an extremely slender basis which is essentially foreign to philosophy.

In fact the roots of this legitimation crisis of philosophy lay at the same level as those of the crisis in art: the earlier harmony between the *task* and the *aptitude for the task* had collapsed. Understandably, philosophy was thus forced to question itself repeatedly, first about the means for its task and then about *the task itself*.

Kant's critical system is the first representative of "sentimental philosophy" (and it is still today representative of it): Kant and Schiller are undoubtedly twin spirits. Kant poses questions about philosophy's aptitude and ability just as much as he does about its task: for him the determination of the limits of the faculties of knowledge — above all of reason — and the limitation of the task occur in a single philosophical movement. According to him, all of philosophy, with the exception of that of Hume, had been naive and uncritical. Certainly, philosophy stemmed from an ineradicable metaphysical need, but this did not mean to say that the need itself can be justified. Kant created the *model* of "sentimental philosophy" without tearing away from philosophy its royal crown. For him, demarcating the limits of philosophy did not mean any *retreat* — neither before science nor before religion. This novel courage of philosophy bled to death at Waterloo — bourgeois philosophy and bourgeois society bade farewell to their heroic epochs at the same time.

Scarcely forty years after Kant's "Copernican deed" Feuerbach was not able to see any difference at all between philosophy before, during and after Kant. According to Feuerbach, all previous philosophies had been "speculative", in that all previous philosophical abstractions took no account of actual people and of the immediacy of humanity itself. For Feuerbach, only one sort of philosophy was possible, namely anthropology — philosophy had to be *reformed again*. Feuerbach's reform suggested two ways forward, both of which were taken up. The first led to existentialism and to "Lebensphilosophie", the second led to the radical philosophy of Marx.

Scarcely ten years after Feuerbach had announced his reform of philosophy, Marx in his theses on Feuerbach characterised all hitherto existing philosophy, including that of Feuerbach, as yet another attempt merely to "explain" the world. Marx demanded that a radically new philosophy should be created which was suited to changing the world. He thereby turned Novalis' aphorism on its head. Questions had to be posed not to philosophy, but to the world: the world had to be changed so that philosophy itself could be transcended. *Not however in that it dissolved itself, but in that it realised itself.*

In his *History and Class Consciousness*, Georg Lukàcs first discovered the related characteristics of the "attitude" of Kant and Schiller. We cannot however share the conclusions that he drew from this.

Lukàcs describes bourgeois consciousness as *total reification* and opposes to it a *totally un-reified* consciousness which he attributes to the proletariat (as represented by an elite). We cannot discuss here how Lukàcs' reception of Marx results from his personal biography. Rather, what appears to be more decisive is his theoretical starting point. Lukàcs posits the total, all-embracing and all-subsuming domination of both Zweckrationalität (purposive rationality in the Weberian sense) and the self-regulating market. If this assumption were proved to be correct, then humanity would be headed towards unavoidable destruction and Lukàcs' theoretical proposal would at least in theory prove to be the only alternative. However, we accept the argument of Karl Polanyi[1] that the notion of society as completely dominated by the self-regulating market is nothing other than the *negative utopia* of bourgeois society. And we can add to this: the totalisation of pure purposive rationality is also no less of a negative utopia.

As we shall see, one of the functions of philosophy is to *de*-fetishise. The generalisation of a completely fetishised consciousness would undoubtedly mean the end of philosophy. And there did in fact exist an historical period in which one could have feared that this was happening: in the nineteenth century philosophy was slumbering in a deep hibernation.

Admittedly, philosophical centuries cannot be measured by the calendar. The heroic century of philosophy died at Waterloo; its twentieth century came into the world in bloody labour during the First World War — the *Tractatus*[2] is the century's prelude.

The nineteenth century is the century of positivism. This is clear if one judges it not by the creation of philosophies, but by their reception. The expression "positivism" itself certainly has changed its meaning. When Marx wrote of the "uncritical positivism" in Hegel's *Philosophy of Law* he did not mean the same thing as contemporary neo-positivism understands by positivism. Nonetheless, this term does have a unitary and inclusive meaning. Whatever form it takes, positivism is the concrete expression of the fetishised bourgeois consciousness. In Hegel this is obscured by the innovative philosophical system which the wonderful edifice of the *Phenomenology* created. Later however this fetishism was openly to reveal itself.

In fact the nineteenth century had no reception of philosophy at all. In this there was no difference between bourgeois and radical philosophy. For the nineteenth century Marx was no philosopher. And just as, as a philosopher, Marx has only been on the agenda since the second decade of our century, so it is also only since that time that Kierkegaard has been appreciated as a philosopher. The twentieth century is an uninterrupted struggle between positivist pseudo-philosophies and genuine philosophies: philosophy is on the point of emerging from its hibernation. This century is on the way to again becoming a "century of philosophy", yet philosophy itself appears not to have noticed this. It seems as if philosophy — including radical philosophy — still suffers from an inferiority complex.

Philosophy is said to be superfluous, because science has stolen its function — philosophy stands on the *defensive*. The response of philosophy is that not *all* its functions have been removed, but only particular ones; it has to change, to become different from what it has been up to now. Philosophy is said to have become superfluous, because immediate action has stepped into its place. And philosophy again goes onto the defensive. The greatest living philosopher [Sartre was still alive when this book was written — AH] of our century *apologises* for being a philosopher and not a mere "fighter"! But the arguments for the "superfluousness" and "impossibility" of philosophy indirectly confirm philosophy. Who would fight against dead gods?

Today nobody would deny that philosophy finds itself in a difficult situation. It is equally difficult to deny that there exists a need for philosophy — a need which is even growing and deepening. Today the social sciences are confronted with questions which are slowly making clear to them that they need philosophy. The scientists do not need philosophy to confirm their methods, since they can achieve these without any philosophy; the activists do not need philosophers who bypass philosophy to fight by their side, since they can fight by themselves without philosophers. However, what is needed is a unitary answer to questions of how one should think, how one should act, how one should live at all, and indeed an answer that is genuinely *philosophical*. And however difficult it may be to be a philosopher, a philosopher's duty is to answer these questions, or at least to do everything possible to give an answer — an answer that is sovereign, autonomous, without self-defence and without excuses.

The time has come for philosophy to become once again committed to itself — and hence to its *own* past and to the truth of its *own* sphere. It is time that philosophy, like Socrates once before, questioned knowledge, asking whether knowledge is true knowledge or mere opinion. It is time for philosophy once again to ask whether it is better to suffer injustice or to commit injustice. It is time for philosophy to take off the clothing that it has merely borrowed, to cease masquerading as natural science or religion, *and to speak its own language*. It is time for philosophy to acknowledge its own structure, which certainly cannot withstand the tests of "critical rationalism", but which is no less true for that and which is, yes, immortal, because it can only die with all of thinking humanity: Sub specie aeternitatis — écrasez l'infâme![3]

2

Philosophy and Need

If one wanted to define more precisely the character and function of philosophy, one could start with those who today are called philosophers, with those who hold chairs in philosophy, or even with the totality of works indexed under the heading "philosophy". Yet of all these only some correspond to the ideas of philosophers or of philosophy. This claim will be developed in what follows.

We understand philosophers to be the representatives of philosophy. We can therefore only understand philosophy's task by starting with philosophy's own world as a sphere of objectification.

Every sphere of objectification satisfies a need of some sort. A sphere of objectification is poly-functional if it can satisfy several needs.[4] The different functions can only be equated with each other if they all can be satisfied through a single objectification. Like art, like scientific theory, and partly like religion, philosophy is an independent and autonomous system of objectification. As such it satisfies needs through its form of reception. One can therefore only discover which of its social functions are primary and which are secondary through an analysis of the types of reception involved.

For this reason in what follows we will discuss first of all *the structure of philosophical expression*, and then the *appropriation of philosophy*.

PHILOSOPHICAL EXPRESSION

The first philosophers, who also created the idea of philosophy, understood philosophy as philosophia, the love of wisdom. Conceptually, wisdom (sophia) contains two aspects: firstly, knowledge, and secondly, upright good conduct, in other words, the True and the Good.[5] The concept of philosophy therefore means the love of the unity between true human knowledge and good human conduct: *the love of the unity of the true and the good.*

The unity of the true and the good is the highest value of philosophy. Consequently philosophy is the love of the highest value. The expression "love" belongs to the vocabulary of the feelings, but it is absolutely in order here. Every philosophy involves feelings: philosophy's feeling is for the good and the true.

Philosophy wants to know *what* the true is and *what* the good is, because philosophy loves the true and the good. It wants to find its Sleeping Beauty, which like a rose is hidden from humanity's sight by a hedge of thorns. It knows that the Sleeping Beauty exists, and it knows that it is also beautiful, yet it does not know what form it takes. As Plato would say, it seeks the Sleeping Beauty in order to recall it, in order to kiss it into life.

The love of the good and the love of the true can be divided. It can happen that the search for the true and the good does not lead to any one *single* truth and to any one *single* good. Already for Aristotle the highest good was a double good: the highest good was the welfare of the state; the highest good was also happiness. Yet all truth and all good are tightly interwoven with one another. Philosophy seeks in all truth *the* true, in all good *the* good, and in all of them the *unity* of both. If it is said that the true and the good are unachievable, or that they do not exist, this does not matter. Even in these cases the conceptual scheme is the same: if the claim is that neither the true nor the good exist, or that still less there exists any unity between them — to confess that the quest is pointless is *still* philosophy.

Philosophy however does not reduce itself to the search for the true and the good or for the unity of them both. It also *finds* them.[6] Philosophies differ above all in terms of *what* they see as incorporating the true and the good or the unity of them both, for the *criteria* can be very different. And it is very largely a question of criteria whether the true and the good are united as identical, whether they are both only "linked", or whether a hierarchy is created between the true and the good. However, if one wants to consider what characterises all philosophies, then one must abstract from the differences between them in the criteria and the hierarchies and start from the criterion that is common to them all — namely that they themselves *constitute* the true and the good they seek. To this extent it not quite true to say that philosophy does not know what form its Sleeping Beauty takes. Since every philosophy seeks *its own* Sleeping Beauty, it knows *quite clearly* what sort it is. Ever since Socrates this has been the well-known irony of philosophy, which characterises all its forms, whether one accepts them or not. Every philosophy searches passionately for the true and the good, and knows from the beginning how to find them (or how not to find them, as in the case of scepticism). Philosophy is also clear — once it begins to search — as to their nature. Philosophy does not know everything, but *from the beginning it knows the ultimate, although it pretends that it is searching for it and knows nothing about it.* This however is neither mystification nor deceit, but instead follows precisely from the highest task of philosophy — it is precisely through this that philosophy fulfils its task.

Philosophy namely *demythologises*. The love of the true and the good is always for it *amor dei intellectualis*. The subject of the passionate recognition of the true and the good is reason: the human being of philosophy is the "rational being". Philosophy opposes to the picturesque ambiguity of mythology the clarity of rational argument. Within the mythological tradition nothing can be questioned; by contrast philosophy demands that *everything* be questioned that its own reason does not understand. Philosophy's pretence that it knows nothing is nothing other than *an invitation to thinking*, to "thinking

together", to thinking with each other. A "philosophical train-
ing" bears the following inscription: "Come, think with me,
let us find the truth together." Philosophers guide people who
think; they lead them with the help of arguments into the clear
light of the true and the good. Philosophical thinking "leads
upwards" to the good and the true. Only in myth can the
Sleeping Beauty be kissed awake *by one person alone*. Yet one
cannot simply point to the Sleeping Beauty and demand:
"There she is. You must love her at once." That is the
language of religion, of revelation. To wake the good and the
true to life, every rational being through its own reason and its
own autonomous thought, with the help of arguments and
counter-arguments, must reach the *same* truth. Without this
there is no philosophy and no philosophical truth. This is the
language of philosophy and hence the attitude of "I know
nothing" belongs to philosophy. Hence we are dealing here
not with deceit, but rather with an organic part of philosophical objectification.

From the point of view of the true and the good every
philosophy is double-sided. One side is that of the philosophical system: philosophers constitute the true and the good and
organise their world accordingly — we will see later how. The
other side is that of the philosophical *attitude*, the systematic
encouragement of co-thinkers to a "summit" which every
rational being can reach.

Let us start with a glance at the first side. "System" here
should not be taken literally. Only a few philosophers *wanted*
to construct a system: what today is described as a system has
usually been reconstructed as such in later times. In what
follows "system" only means that every philosophy possesses
its own world in which every thought and every argument can
only be interpreted *within the whole*, because they all relate to
the whole.

A philosophical system is always founded on the tension
between what *Is* and what *Ought* to be — it is this which
characterises the philosophical system and which brings it to
its fullest expression. The unity of the true and the good is the
"Ought-to-be". Philosophy always arranges what merely *is*

from the point of view of what *ought to be* — the ought (the true unity of the good and the true) is the measure by which the reality or unreality of being is assessed. Defetishism is therefore a feature of philosophical systems from the beginning. What else can the dissolution of prejudices be, other than a questioning of what is, from the point of view of what ought to be?

Certain philosophers have defined what ought-to-be as "essence" in contrast to the "phenomenal" nature or the "appearance" of mere being. Frequently too, appearance and essence are ascribed to different *cognitive abilities*: until the appearance of empiricism this was nearly always the case. Within philosophy "essence" should not occur as an ontological factor, and further, cognitive abilities should not be classified in relation to how "appearance" and "essence" are understood. Nonetheless, the "essential" and the "inessential" are always present in relation to the interpretation of *reality* in some form. Namely, for every philosophy what ought to be counts as *the most real*: nothing can be more real than the true and the good or the unity of the two. To this extent the common commitment of philosophies is *ens perfectissimum — ens realissimum*. What ought to be is no illusion of fantasy, no mere dream only present in our subjective wishes, bur rather the "Ought-to-be" is precisely what matters, the measure, "the true" or "the most real reality". What ought to be has so to speak a "topographical location". In metaphysics this is either the "heights" or the "depths", in certain social philosophers it lies in ideal institutions, in Kant it is in humanity itself — in freedom, in free will as *the factum* of reason; others see it in a *mode of behaviour* or in the relationship to what exists (as for example in Heidegger, who contrasts authentic being with inauthentic being).

Every philosophy constitutes in a different way its Ought, its *that which is most real for it*. Yet this much is clear: this Ought, however it may be constituted, is either something that is *general* or something that is *indivisible* and that cannot be subdivided into anything more particular (in the period in which the specific philosophy emerges). The idea that is seen to be particular cannot ever be the Ought of philosophy. This notion is inherent in philosophy as a form of thought and can be seen to be present in philosophy from its very beginning. Philosophy could *not* remain stationary at the establishment of the four elements: either water or fire or infinitude had to incoporate everything, or the atom, the indivisible element, had to become the fundament of everything. One finds the same in the heyday of "sentimental philosophy": for Kant humankind is the universal — the personality is humanity itself within every human being, while for Feuerbach humanness is the singular — the concrete, *individual* sensuous being.

The most individual or the most general, the birthplaces of the good and the true or of the unity of both, are what ought to be and what is at the same time most real, the ens realissimum. A glance at the history of philosophy suffices to see that this connection characterises every "philosophical world" and every philosophical system. Plato opposed to the world of the shadows the world of ideas; Aristotle opposed to matter pure form; Spinoza discovered in the substance the true and the good and what at the same time was most real, with every individual existence being only an manifestation of this substance; Rousseau confronted the empirical world of the volonté de tous with the essential reality of the volonté générale; Kant contrasted *homo phenomenon* with *homo noumenon*, the former being the source of all evil, the latter the source of good; in Hegel humanity is, also unconsciously, a means for the "self-realisation" of the world spirit; Marx contrasts to alienated humanity the "species being" and to "all hitherto existing history" *true* history; for Kierkegaard the inessentiality of the aesthetic, and the banality of the moral stage, is opposed by the truth and the "knight of faith" who transcends everyday custom; Lukács' *History and Class Consciousness* is constructed from the contrast of empirical consciousness with imputed consciousness; in Wittgenstein's tragic philosophy one should keep silent about the most true, the good.

What ought to be is therefore the confrontation of what is most real with what is. Between Ought and Is there is a *tension.* The brier hides by its facticity the Sleeping Beauty. Yet what is is itself constituted by what ought to be. Only in the light of the essence, only in the light of what ought to be, is what is inessential. Hamlet expresses this paradox in immortal fashion: "There is nothing either good or bad, but thinking makes it so."[1]

To this paradox is added another, one which shows that the philosophical system and the philosophical attitude do not stand in a purely external relationship to each other. Neither can exist without the other: together they *mean* philosophy.

For philosophy constructs its world, as we have shown, with *rational argument*. Something is only true for philosophy if every thinking person can recognise it to be true with the help of their own reason. Philosophy's function is, with the help of rational thought, to lead rational human beings to the recognition of what ought to be — that good and true which philosophy already knows. This "leading upwards" is the core of the philosophical system and of the "world" of philosophy.

Therefore on the one hand what is is constituted from what ought to be, on the other hand however what ought to be must be *deduced* from what is, otherwise it would not be possible for every thinking person from the world of what is to be led up to what ought to be. Even Kant, who knew very well that this hurdle existed, did not retreat before it, for philosophy *cannot retreat from it*. To "lead up" to the categorical imperative he needed the *fact of conscience* as *something that existed*.

Yet is this really a "hurdle"? Can one consider as a "hurdle" to philosophy that which forms its essence? Can one treat as a "hurdle" to philosophy the fact that it is *utopian*?

The "utopian spirit" is the spirit of philosophy. Every philosophy is utopian — how else could one describe a construction in which that which ought to be counts as the most real of all that exists, where whatever is counts as unreal in the light of the ultimate reality, and yet the former is deduced from the latter? In that it does this, philosophy is not merely any utopia, but a *rational utopia*. If this only meant that philosophy proffered its Ought — its ultimate reality — as knowledge, then one could speak of a pseudo-rationality.

However philosophy does not consist only of this. Philosophy offers its utopia to those who think autonomously, to those who are disciplined and systematic thinkers. This utopia really is *knowledge*, not just the appearance of knowledge.

Whoever claims that the rationality of philosophy is mere appearance (since what ought to be cannot be deduced from what is, and anyway philosophy only deduces what it already knows), measures philosophy by a non-philosophical criterion. This overlooks that the real *function of deduction* is the *"leading upwards"*. Doubtless for philosophy the leading upwards to the unity of what is and what ought appears as primary; doubtless the chain of reasoning is often broken when it deduces from what is. When in Plato's *Politeia* truth can find no more arguments in the world of being, although it knows itself to be the true, there then follows the "leap" into the transcendental. When Spinoza confirms that one calls good what is useful and then on the contrary asserts that what is useful is what is good, he clearly makes himself guilty of logical inconsistency. This however is a *fruitful* inconsistency of philosophy, for it follows from the *essence*, from the utopian character of philosophy.

Every utopia confronts what is with some or other criterion. The differentia specifica of a rational utopia lies in the nature of this criterion. This criterion is, as we know, the unity of the true and the good. One can only approach the true with the question "What is truth?" "What is truth?" poses the question of cognitive *reason*, the question posed by people who want to *know* — not only glimpse, feel or suspect — what truth is.

When Christ declared that he was the truth, Pilate asked him what then truth was. His question was irrelevant, for the two were talking past each other. Christ spoke the language of religion, Pilate the language of philosophy. The religious utopia involves revelation — in it there is no higher claim than "I am the truth". One cannot however answer the question "What is truth?" with "I am the truth". The answer can only be, consider, reflect, we want to seek the truth together; the philosophical utopia demands the thinking cognition of the rational being. Therefore the rational utopia necessarily contains the philosophical *attitude*.

Plato made his Socrates express practically every aspect of this attitude. In all cases its starting point is that of *astonishment* ("taumadzein"). This astonishment at the world already contains a moment of de-fetishism, for it means simply that one puts into question what is self-evident — that one precisely does not accept it as self-evident. Doubtless astonishment ("taumadzein") is an aspect of every theoretical orientation, but in philosophy it is more — it creates a way of observing reality which is capable of eliminating from consciousness all prejudices and all existing inherited knowledge. For philosophy knowledge that already exists is mere "opinion" and this, precisely because it already exists, *cannot* be the starting point of the "leading upwards". In Hume's time it was self-evident that a causal chain linked all natural phenomena. For his part Hume dissolved this "self-evident" fact by questioning it — that is astonishment ("taumadzein"). In Marx's time money and commodity relations appeared as self-evident. Marx stressed this "self-evidentness" and questioned it: behind the reified relations one should seek the human relations! That too is astonishment ("taumadzein"). Husserl's "phenomenological reduction" turns this philosophical attitude — admittedly from the perspective of a *particular philosophy* — into the methodological foundation of cognition.

It is certainly utopian to posit a naive consciousness, one that is purified of all prejudices, one that is astonished at the world and one that questions everything. Certainly philosophy often plays the role of Andersen's child hero, often crying "The emperor has no clothes!" And yet for the naive astonishment ("taumadzein") of philosophy there are limiting conditions with two interrelated aspects. Firstly, the representative of philosophy is the philosopher and, to repeat a commonplace, such a person is always a child of their time and a bearer of the needs, judgements and prejudices of their historical period, even when they most determinedly attack its "preconceived knowledge" and its prejudices. Two things however make astonishment ("taumadzein") possible. On the one hand, the philosopher has the ability to choose autonomously between the thoughts and values prescribed by the spirit of the time and to be on the lookout for available alternatives. On the other hand, the philosopher creates a consciousness that is in the position to *think through to the end* what in the time is *thinkable* at all and what the average person has not thought through to the end. Secondly, philosophers are not usually capable of abstracting from the conceptions and the questions of *past philosophers*. At minimum they will react to them in the form of negation. Precisely the feature of a rational utopia, that it is founded on *knowledge*, unavoidably demands confrontation with the knowledge that has gone before, whether this be in the form of acceptance, reworking, or criticism. Unlike the "utopian reality" of art, philosophy cannot simply cut itself off from its past.

At the same time however, and even if this sounds paradoxical, every philosophy takes as its "beginning" astonishment ("taumadzein"), the "norm" of preconceptionless consciousness, in order to construct on this basis its system, its world. And here too one can once again observe the organic linkage between the philosophical attitude and the philosophical system. This construction, always beginning from the same starting point, clings to the unique duplicity of the philosophical "world". On the one hand every philosophical system is *independent* — a unique, unrepeatable and inimitable temple of rationality. Everything from the foundations to the spire[8] is its inalienable *property*. Every philosophical system is an *individuality*: from this perspective there is no development in philosophy. On the other hand every philosophical system is based on knowledge and *must* therefore work on what it has inherited from its predecessors. In the same way it must reflect the general development of human knowledge, or at least it cannot contradict this growing knowledge. To this extent philosophies do, so to speak, build on each other and philosophical *development does exist*.

The way "taumadzein" is the foundation stone of philosophy is also shown in that it certainly is the starting point of every philosophy, but every philosophy makes clear *which* prejudices, *which* opinions, *which* contents of false consciousness must be abstracted from in order to see the world "naively". Doubtless however the direction in which this transcendence of prejudices occurs is itself determined by prejudices. Bacon names four idols from which understanding must be purged so that it can be astonished at the world free from preconceptions — Descartes, Spinoza and the whole philosophy of the Enlightenment proceed in exactly the same way. Rousseau *knows* that civilisation corrupts understanding. Even sentimental philosophy, which banishes astonishment ("taumadzein") from its *construction*, admits to *its own taumadzein*. What else is the waking from the dogmatic dream but the questioning of everything self-evident, the refusal to understand as natural what for long counted as natural?

Astonishment ("taumadzein") does not however exhaust the philosophical attitude. Philosophy possesses the wonderful ability and the courage to *pose childish questions*: "What is that?" "What is that for?" "Why is that like that?" "Why must that be like that?" "What purpose has that?" "Why must that be done like that?" "Why cannot one act like that?"

Someone who claims that they "know everything" will angrily respond to these childish questions: "Everyone knows that." "Because it's like that and that's it." "Because everyone does it like that." "Don't ask so many questions." Philosophers however *insist on posing childish questions*, for they are the soil in which they can sow the seed of *their* knowledge from which the first beginnings of their system grow into full maturity. We have already seen that the philosopher's "I know that I know nothing" is meant ironically, yet at the same time this irony is only relative. Philosophers have only *become* philosophers in that they have been able to pose childish questions themselves and therefore know that the seeds of philosophy must be sown in this soil, and only in this soil.

The childish questions contain two aspects: on the one hand the knowledge of unknowledge, the lack of preconceptions, the questioning of existing prejudices, and on the other hand the thirst for knowledge and understanding. It is therefore no accident that philosophy is always above all addressed to *youth*. Even the most vehement controversies amongst philosophers are only rarely intended to convince other philosophers. Instead, philosophers compete with each other over pure "uncorrupted" youth. Plato's Socrates wants to convince of his truth not *Trasymachos*, but rather *Glaukon*. *Youth is philosophy's earthly love*, for philosophy sees and develops in it the ability to recognise the good, the beautiful and the true: youth has openness, thirst for knowledge, and if it does not entirely lack preconceptions, then at least its prejudices have not yet hardened and can still open a path to the free and autonomous use of reason.

Philosophy is convinced of the high value of its knowledge; it is usually also convinced that it wears the crown of the sciences. At the same time it is *in its essence* to offer a knowledge that can be appropriated by anyone who is prepared for *mental endeavour*: no philosophy permits any doubt that "leading upwards" involves mental effort. "To be appropriated by everyone" means that philosophical thinking demands *no* pre-existing knowledge; precisely for this reason it can be grasped by the "uncorrupted reason" of youth. Indeed, we have already pointed out that a philosophical system cannot exclude the knowledge of preceding philosophies, and that it cannot reject the knowledge (incorporated in other objectifications) of its time. Many philosophers were distinguished by their encyclopaedic knowledge, but yet they did not assume such a knowledge in those whom they wanted to "lead upwards" to their own philosophy. Kant, who was legendary for his knowledge, declared that the categorical imperative could be explained without any trouble to a ten-year-old child. Even the most complicated philosophical terminology is constructed in such a way that it can — at least in its starting point — be grasped and comprehended merely by *reflection*. Yet, whoever has acquired these categories can, on the basis of this knowledge, proceed to the next stages.

Certainly philosophy came into the world in the *agora*[9] — it is a child of the democracy of the *polis*. The first philosopher got an ignorant slave to deduce the Pythagoran theorem; the first radical philosopher discovered in the German working class its "great theoretical sense".

We have said that philosophy — every philosophy — can be

understood by anyone who is prepared for mental endeavour. However, this formulation puts a question mark after the democratic nature of philosophy. After all, we know that the majority of humanity (apart from very short episodes in its history) has never even come close to the mere *possibility* of such readiness. It is generally known that since the time of the Enlightenment philosophy has absorbed this contradiction into itself and made itself conscious of it. Since the Enlightenment it has been the guiding idea of every genuine philosophy that every human *should* be capable of mental endeavour in the same way as everyone *should* have the same desire for true knowledge.

We have seen that it is a characteristic feature of philosophy to sow already ripened seeds in the unprejudiced thought of youth, so that there they grow into autonomous thinking. This also makes philosophers into *teachers*. And in fact philosophers do have schoolmasterly traits. They build argument upon argument, they discipline thinking, they attempt to eradicate all ambiguities. As schoolmasters, they may in certain circumstances appear pedantic, but they shape their relationship to their pupils in the spirit of philosophy — that is, democratically. Because of the fact that they are both beings equipped with reason, teacher and pupil are always equal. This applies just as much when the teacher is a ruler, as for example Marcus Aurelius, as when the pupil is a ruler, as for example Alexander the Great. The leading upwards into philosophy is not the introduction to a trade. Philosophy is not an occupation, and to be guided into the philosophical system consists far more in the philosophical orientation being turned into methodical and rational thinking — a shaping from the perspective of the unity of the good and the true, of the Is and the Ought. The pupils do not have to become philosophers, but must actively appropriate philosophy — this possibility of appropriation exists for all pupils of philosophy, whatever their occupation. Philosophers do not want to train just future philosophers, but rather everyone. For everyone is, like them, a *rational being*.

All this shows how important in the history of philosophy is the founding of "schools". The school is the activity of philosophers. For teachers, pupils who have grown up are their greatest confirmation, and for philosophers their greatest confirmation is those pupils who have surpassed them, even if they have also turned against their masters (assuming all the time that they are guided by the love of the good and the true).

The connection between the philosophical system and the philosophical attitude must also be seen from *another perspective*. It has already been said that philosophy is a rational utopia constructed from the tension between what is and what ought to be: the good, the true and — although not always — the beautiful. Philosophy demands thinking and through thinking leads up to its world. Philosophy is a summons to thinking, hence a summons to perceive the true *and* the good as a unity. This can be succinctly summarised as: "Consider how you should think; consider how you should act; consider how you should live." "How you should live" involves "how you should think" and "how you should act". Philosophy as a rational utopia is always the utopia of a *form of life*. To this extent Kant expressed the "secret" of all philosophies (including contemplative philosophy): this "secret" is nothing other than the *primacy of practical reason. The highest good* always comprises the goal of utopia as a mode of life. The system *is only true* if it reveals *the highest good*. The philosopher has to vouch for the highest good.

Certainly all philosophers have to convert their *own* philosophy into their own attitude to life. For Socrates the will of the *polis*, the city state, was an incontestable value: if he had fled he would have destroyed his own philosophy's credibility. Aristotle placed the contemplative life above public activity: therefore when his life was endangered he could flee from his adopted homeland without any hesitation and not rob his philosophy of authenticity. One cannot condemn Kant as a philosopher because he never experienced love: his philosophy did not contain love and so did not lose its persuasive power because of this lack in the philosopher. One cannot criticise Hobbes, the fanatic for the idea of the state, because he supported whatever state was strongest, for that *followed* from his own philosophy, just as loneliness dedicated to the *amor dei intellectualis* followed from Spinoza's own philosophy. Kierkegaard *could not* marry Regine Olsen, for he could not choose for himself a form of life which he tried to reject in his own philosophy.

When in the Introduction we claimed that today philosophy has become difficult, we certainly also meant by this the constitution of the good and the true, but not primarily. What today has become difficult is the philosophical *attitude*, and in different ways. Today philosophy is incorporated in the social division of labour: objectification basically is *not a job*, yet it has *become* a job. If this merely had the result that those who carried out the philosophical "job" were not all philosophers, or even if the majority of them were not philosophers, then we could not speak of a *real* problem. The real problem lies in the fact that for genuine philosophy it has become a labour of Sisyphus to emancipate itself from the limitation of philosophy as a "job". With a few exceptions, philosophers today are only allowed to be *teachers* when they are "professors". As professors, they must submit both to the demands of the division of labour which is incorporated in institutions, and to the expectations of the "discipline". Their philosophical task consists in the creation of astonishment ("taumadzein"), in the development of the ability to think autonomously, in "leading upwards", in ironic commitment to "I know nothing". However, this task conflicts with the requirements of the "job" and with the need to pass on "positive knowledge" — and nothing contradicts more the ironic starting point of "I know nothing" than this. Philosophers must live their philosophy, otherwise it is not authentic: philosophy is a form of life. The framework of philosophers' lives — and hence of their form of life — is now firmly located in the division of labour between the disciplines. However, what is difficult is not impossible. It is the *duty* of philosophers — today no less than in other periods of history — to live according to their philosophy; they must face the risk of conflict with the "job" and with the division of labour itself, for these rob philosophy of its effectiveness, of its real function, of its democratic character. To doubt the validity of the philosophical division of labour is an integral part of the dissolution of prejudices and hence an integral part of philosophy. Anyone who will not face this conflict should be a cobbler, and not a philosopher.

If we in fact claim that the task of philosophy is difficult, then we have merely said that *even today* philosophy still has a difficult task. "More difficult" is only correct in that there is one way in which the task of philosophy is actually more burdensome than before. Today it is necessary to have *self-awareness* of the difficulty of philosophy, and hence of the difficulty of overcoming the controls of the "job" — the bulwarks of repressive tolerance.

The task of philosophy was always complicated, but in the times before repressive tolerance philosophy was itself aware of this. "Danger" was the "natural condition" of philosophy. This is also self-evident, for philosophy is *always* about *enlightenment*, and it was so before the word "enlightenment" was coined. In that it appeals to human beings to "think with your own head", it always wants to free humanity from its condition of "self-imposed immaturity". Philosophy has no power, yet the powerful fear nothing more than people who do think with their own heads. From the perspective of the rational utopia of the highest good, the facticity of what exists is untrue, un-good, inauthentic, nothing but appearance, nothing but illusion: its confirmation is not knowledge, but mere opinion. Therefore philosophy is *dangerous* in the eyes of every representative and defender of facticity; they point the finger at philosophy: "Écrasez l'infâme!"[10]

Philosophy is dangerous; to represent philosophy is dangerous; to be a philosopher is dangerous. Those condemned to death: Socrates, Bruno and the others; those robbed of their freedom: Boethius, Abelard, Diderot and the others; the exiles and those who went voluntarily into exile: Protagoras, Aristotle, Descartes, Hobbes, Marx and the others; those thrust into isolation, the accused, the threatened: Rousseau, Kant, Fichte and the others . . . And the "lucky ones": Plato sold as a slave, Spinoza excommunicated, Leibniz unable to publish his chief work, Hegel's best pupil imprisoned, Feuerbach forgotten, Kierkegaard destroyed by a slander campaign.

In many parts of the world today the defenders of facticity attack philosophy in the spirit of pseudo-religious intolerance. In these regions it is *just as* difficult to be a philosopher as in the time of Descartes or Spinoza. Where however the defence of facticity takes the form of "specialised knowledge", then philosophy even acquires a new status. It then has to *fight for* its own dangerousness. Indeed it has to do this against a new form of fetishism that befriends it. This form is all the more friendly since philosophy itself struggles for *knowledge*: for the philosopher who searches for true knowledge it is doubtless more difficult to be accused of being "unscientific" than to be accused of being an "unbeliever". To oppose fetishised knowledge requires courage, perhaps a new form of courage. Yet whoever traces their ancestry from Socrates *ought* to know to what this *commits* them.

Every philosophical construction therefore expresses an obligatory form of life which its creator formulates as genuine knowledge. It is one of the most noticeable characteristics of philosophical systems that in this way they reflect the personality of their authors. Philosophy never *intends* to be expressive, indeed quite the opposite: philosophers always want to hide behind their philosophy and present not *their* truth, but "the truth". The paradox however is precisely that the more philosophers try to crawl away behind their thoughts, the more their life work expresses their personality. In any philosophy one perceives so strong a portrait of the whole person that in the history of philosophy (unlike in the history of art) the investigation of so-called biographical factors is almost irrelevant. One "sees the individuals" and does not need to know anything more about them. It is easier for even music and poetry to be merely combinations of conventional elements of "ordinary speech" than it is for philosophy. It is possible to play roles in poetry, but *there is no role-playing in philosophy*. Every philosophy has autobiographical traits.

Certainly this is a paradox. For there is no philosophical system that *would not make an unconditional claim to its own truth*. In order to declare love for someone, one does not have to consider the object of love as necessarily perfect. Philosophy demystifies what is from the perspective of what ought to be — the perspective of the good and the true. But there is one thing that it does not question — *itself*. Above all, astonishment ("taumadzein") is only the starting point: it only purifies understanding to enable the reception of the system, but the system itself cannot be built on this. Every philosophy searches for a pivot — if necessary, for several pivots — on which the system can be constructed so that it is unconditionally true. Each philosophy does not consider this fixed point merely as the pivot of its *own* system. It assumes that, proceeding from this point, it — and only it — can "find" the truth and therefore is in possession of the highest knowledge. Accordingly, it also assumes that this starting point is the *guaranteed source* of all true human cognition. Each philosophy therefore wishes its foundation to be the foundation of *all* knowledge along the lines of: the source of all knowledge is sensual experience, or, the ultimate fixed point is the evidence of thinking, or, the basis of all cognition is an a priori synthetic judgement.

However, the "truth" of philosophy involves not only the "true", but also the good, for even the true is subordinated to the highest good. In the highest good "manifest themselves" whatever were the highest values of the philosophers of any period. Each philosopher *chooses* this guiding value from the stock of existing values and invests it with a unique meaning and a unique importance. These values acquire their unique meaning and importance from the structure of the system: they can be interpreted in one way, and in one way only *within the system*. Since however the philosophy is convinced that it has tracked down the truth, and since it knows what form this takes, it posits the universal validity of the highest good in the meaning in which it expresses it and "deduces" this meaning with the help of a chain of rational arguments.

Antiquity was unanimous in its belief that happiness was the highest good. Then along came the philosophers to explain that happiness meant this and that, happiness meant not this but that, happiness meant neither that nor that but this. The highest good of modern times is undoubtedly freedom. Then the philosophers came to explain that freedom could be nothing other than the love of God, freedom could be nothing other than obedience to the laws, nothing other than obedience to one's *own* laws, nothing other than the will to good, nothing other than the recognition of necessity, nothing other than the transcendence of alienation, nothing other than our existence itself. And when philosophers now and then concede that other philosophers' concept of freedom has "some sort of sense" to it, they immediately go on to prove that that freedom represents an historically transcended or "lower" stage and that it is only a subordinate, accidental and limited concept in comparison to their *true and genuine* concept of freedom.

Every philosophy is convinced that with the help of its own particular "solid" starting point its form of construction has justified both this same starting point and its method of cognition. It also believes that the highest good which it has constituted forms the basis of all values. These claims are therefore the *false consciousness* of philosophy, but this does not however mean that philosophy is the representative of this "false consciousness". This blemish belongs to the nature of philosophy, but philosophy *corrects it itself*, in that there is not one philosophy but rather *philosophies*. The history of philosophy is a history of philosophical *polemics*.

Every philosophy claims a universal validity for itself in that at the same time it also questions the truth of *other* philosophies. Every philosophy constitutes itself through the critique of another system or of other systems. Philosophical critique is always aimed at the totality of the philosophy that is being criticised. The critique never limits itself to the refutation of particular details but always attacks the "neuralgic points" of the other philosophy. These "neuralgic points" however always form the *centre* of the philosophy: its basis of cognition, the way it defines the meaning of the highest good. Sometimes one and sometimes the other is the target of the critique, but usually both are.

Every philosophy can only constitute itself if it exposes the false consciousness of *another* philosophy. Although it itself does this with false consciousness, its own false consciousness will be exposed by another philosophy and this in turn by a third.

Every philosophy offers a form of life; every philosophy is the critique of a form of life and at the same time the advocacy of another form of life. The new system and the new form of life already form the starting point of the critique. Thus Plato polemicised against the Sophists, Aristotle against Plato, the Platonists of the Renaissance against Aristotle, Descartes against Aristotle and the philosophy of the Renaissance; thus Hobbes, Descartes and Gassendi polemicised against each other, Spinoza against Descartes, Leibniz against Spinoza and Locke, Hume against Hobbes, Kant against all metaphysics, Diderot, Rousseau and Voltaire against each other, Voltaire against Leibniz, Feuerbach against Hegel, Marx against Hegel and Feuerbach.

What however does it mean when we say that critique is the advocacy of another mode of life and at the same time the exposure of the false consciousness of the philosophy that is being criticised? Quite simply, it means that the controversy over the truth or falsity of a philosophy is unavoidably also a *discussion of values*. For when one philosophy criticises another philosophy and perceives its false consciousness, then it criticises it as *untrue* in that it confronts its value with another.

We cannot consider this as "refutation" in the normal sense of the word. The critique does not "refute" the other philosophy but *rejects it and moves away from it*. And this applies even in the case when the critique corresponds to every formal criterion of refutation.

We will return later to the forms of philosophical controversy, but for the moment only one thing needs to be remembered. Philosophers do not primarily address other philosophers; philosophies struggle over the "uncorrupted" souls — reception is the confirmation of philosophy. From the point of view of the recipients however, the world of philosophy is just as pluralist as the world of art. All recipients see themselves as facing not "philosophy" but "philosophies", each of which offers *another* version of the true and the good, *another* form of life. If however recipients choose a philosophy, and with its logic and with the help of their own reason autonomously think it through to the end, then however much this philosophy may have been criticised and however many of its adherents it may have lost, they are and will remain true to it.

Aristotle provides the proof that the theory of ideas is false for he advocated another form of life. After him however it was still *possible* to return to the theory of ideas. This process was often to be repeated. Stoicism and Epicureanism arose in the ancient world, but nonetheless people have chosen them again and again: *we too* can choose them. Hegel confirmed this: one cannot learn to swim without jumping into the water and in this way he advocated another form of life. That however does not prevent anyone from returning to Kant, something that happened continually and which still happens today. Let us try however to imagine that someone wishes to return to Ptolemy. His system is refuted — it does not exist any more, it cannot be chosen. Copernican meditations cannot be written in the twentieth century, yet by contrast Cartesian meditations are perfectly possible. We will have to discuss again the fact that this "return" is never a return *to the same thing* or a return *in the same way*. Nonetheless in this regard the pluralism of philosophy does not differ at all from that of art, except in one respect. Given the logical and rational structure of philosophy, the moment of return is always *more explicit* and involves fewer illusions than in the case of art.

The false self-consciousness of philosophy is therefore always put into question by the history of philosophy itself. Without this false consciousness however there would be no philosophy — it belongs to it like the skin to the body. Those who point out the inessential nature of mere facticity can only do so if they claim for themselves the status "sub specie aeternitatis". The world however continually needs this "écrasez l'infâme" — this questioning of the self-evident, this doubting of facticity, this exposure of mere opinions, this confrontation of autonomy with heteronomy, in short this confrontation of utopia (as what is rational) with what exists

(as what has to be overthrown or overcome). We must therefore also accept this false consciousness of philosophy, this
"sub specie aeternitatis", without which there could be no
"écrasez l'infâme", and therefore no questioning of what is
self-evident.

THE APPROPRIATION OF PHILOSOPHY

Philosophical objectifications suggest to the recipient: "Consider how you should think; consider how you should act;
consider how you should live." In their creation these three
moments are one and indivisible, but it is *possible* that they can
be relatively separate in their reception. Doubtless the reception of philosophy is as varied as there are recipients of philosophy, but nonetheless it is essential to delimit and classify the
main *types* of reception. Only so can we demonstrate both that
philosophy is *multi-functional* and that the different types of
reception all indicate the existence of a common need.

Before analysing the types of reception we must make clear
that we do not consider the way the so-called "discipline of
philosophy" tackles philosophy to be a reception of *philosophy*
at all. In fact, this way of tackling philosophy does not stem
from the need for philosophy; its purpose is not the function
of philosophy. For the "discipline of philosophy", as in so
many other disciplines, philosophy is merely "research
material". Philologists certainly know better than all philosophers put together which terminology appears how often and
in what context in the Corpus Aristotelicum, but such knowledge is hardly a genuine appropriation of Aristotelian philosophy. Cultural historians may find in the philosophy of the
Middle Ages countless references without these having for
them any other value than as references from different docu-
ments in the archives. This is not to question the achievement
of cultural historians and their like, but it is to challenge the
assumption that all of this has the slightest relationship to the
fact that the material or object which is being worked on is
actually philosophy. The problem does not lie in the fact that

members of separate disciplines use philosophical works or philosophical *and other* works to create the subject-matter and the source of their knowledge. The problem is rather that these experts who approach philosophy as a discipline are described and understood as philosophers. The "confusion" between experts and philosophers certainly merely demonstrates that philosophy is subordinated to the social division of labour, even though it actually does not have the character of a discipline or an occupation. The "philosophical experts" have no philosophy themselves, although they know about every philosophy: the philosophies are part of the knowledge of their discipline. Since they have no philosophy, for them it is not a form of life and one cannot demand from them any unity of thought and conduct.

We have already mentioned how much the task of philosophy is hampered by its incorporation in the scientific and social division of labour. To the philosophical attitude (the "taumadzein") the "job" is a thorn in the flesh. All the petty bureaucrats of the discipline get themselves certified as philosophers by hiding their *ignorance* under a jungle of footnotes. The genuine philosophers by contrast have the difficult task of hiding their *knowledge* behind a maze of footnotes — they have to fortify their new thoughts and their new points of view with "academic references" so that they will not be condemned as "dilettantes" or, even worse, as *plagiarists*. In reality plagiarism is *foreign* to genuine philosophy. The ancients knew that — they liberally poured out philosophical thoughts in speech and in writing to other philosophers without "worrying" that their thoughts would be stolen from them. How could anybody steal someone else's *personality*? Philosophically therefore, the footnote is suspect. And this, not only because no philosophical system is made better, more true or more beautiful by making the work of the recipient more difficult with a flood of references, but also because the footnote is a sign of "possessive individualism". It is the manifestation of the fact that now thought too is subsumed under the categories of "yours" and "mine" — like a house, a cow or a wife — and is no longer "ours".

However, to return to categorising the types of philosophical recipient. In the case of those types of reception which incorporate all three aspects of a philosophy (consider how you should think, consider how you should act and consider how you should live) we speak of a *complete reception*, whereas in the cases of those which include only the first, the second, or the third aspect we speak of a *partial reception*. In the case of the complete reception the appropriation of the philosophical objectification results from the *intention* being directed towards the objectification. In the case of a partial reception the intention is not invested in the philosophical objectification itself, for here philosophical reception is a *means to another end* — from the solution of problems of personal life through to the formation of theories in other areas. We will see later that in the case of a "preferential", that is, partial, reception, this too does not occur in complete isolation from the other aspects.

There are three types of complete reception: that of the aesthete, that of the connoisseur and that of the truly philosophical recipient. Anyone who receives philosophy *aesthetically* appropriates a philosophical work through its *form*. The form of a philosophical work is not identical with the philosophical system involved: one and the same philosophical system is often constructed through a series of philosophical works, each one formed and structured in the same way. At the same time, however, every philosophical work that has been thought through to the end has a form that is *adequate* to it. It is not easy for philosophers to find this form that is adequate to the thought: it involves no less effort than it does for artists. Since however philosophy wishes to form a *thought* adequately, the best form will prove to be the one which is most suitable to the unfolding of the thought, which orders what is from the perspective of what ought to be and which makes the deduction of what ought to be from what is as clear and as transparent as possible. We know that a philosophical work is just as individual as a work of art and that it expresses the personality of its creator — the more so the less that this is intended. In philosophy a form of life and the outlook on life that is embedded in it are transformed into a logical chain of thought. It is therefore self-evident that through the appropriation of the form by the recipient the work itself can become a form of life, an experience, an outlook on life.

The fact that a philosophical work is formed does not necessarily mean that it has to be "poetic". It *can* be poetic, like for example the dialogues of Plato or the work of Kierkegaard. Yet a dry and didactic construction can also constitute philosophical form. *The Critique of Pure Reason* is a completely formed philosophical work; if we claim that it is "beautiful" then this is not meant in the usual sense of the word. Yet anyone who after reading Spinoza's *Ethic* or Hegel's *Phenomenology of Mind* has never had the feeling of "beauty" has no musical sense for philosophical form.

Certainly the aesthetic recipient is not the only person to experience the "beauty" of a philosophical work. For us, aesthetic recipients are those who approach philosophical work as primarily something beautiful, with the result that their reception will always be *cathartic*. Thought affects them not primarily as thought, but as *feeling*. The aesthetic reception presupposes no general knowledge of philosophical problems or of philosophical polemics. The object of the aesthetic reception can be a *single* philosophical work which is read over and over again — as a novel can be.

The fact that aesthetic reception does not primarily stimulate further thoughts, and so does not "transpose" the philosophical work, in no way contradicts the claim that this is a complete reception, for at the same time the feeling that is released in catharsis is a world view. Aesthetic recipients do not seek in philosophy an answer to the problems of their own life, but rather an answer to the problem of "life" in general. For them the reception of form means: "I've found it! One should think *thus*, act thus, live thus."[11] The reception opens up to them an *interpretation of the world*. That catharsis involves feelings merely means that aesthetic recipients have no *critical relationship* to the work that is received. They feel: "This is true and one must think thus, one cannot think any other way." Reception is not followed by any further astonishment ("taumadzein") and the clarity cannot be reversed.

For the connoisseurs philosophy is a part of culture. They

consciously appropriate philosophy as an organic part of human culture. They understand and interpret philosophical systems in their entirety and primarily admire in them the human achievement. The connoisseur has philosophical "good taste", an intuitive sense of the differences between the achievements of philosophies: connoisseurs provide the basic circle of those who understand, judge and read philosophies. The canonisation of the philosophies occurs through the common sense of the connoisseurs. Obviously the common sense of the connoisseurs of one period can — as is always the case with common sense — be altered and modified by the common sense of the connoisseurs of subsequent periods. How large the number of the "connoisseurs" of philosophy is, and how actively they participate in the formation of the philosophical public, always depends on how "philosophically" the basic thought of a particular time is structured. One regrettable fact of the current stage of development of philosophy is precisely that one cannot speak of any significant number of connoisseurs. This doubtless is linked to the "disciplinary specialisation" of philosophy. Someone like Kant could explain the core idea of his philosophical system to "unknown" connoisseurs and give great weight to their "good taste". Today even the categorisation of philosophies in terms of their importance is a "private affair" of the specialist philosophers, so that it is hardly surprising that these specialists, who have absolutely nothing of "the true" and "the good" to offer the world of humanity, have incredibly high prestige. Since however the laity have no possibility of becoming "connoisseurs", their judgements are not an expression of common sense but count far more as "sensation". The competent judgement of the achievements of philosophy is now replaced partly by the prestige of sterile specialist knowledge and partly by the prestige of fashion.

Philosophical recipients are the *real* recipients of philosophy. They appropriate philosophy *philosophically*. They *choose* a philosophy and always only one philosophy. They therefore choose a rational utopia — a form of life. For precisely this reason it is also their duty to live this philosophy. They also have to commit themselves to the categorical imperative of philosophy ("Live your life as your philosophy dictates!") and to follow it.

The philosophical reception of a philosophy is based on *interpretation*. The recipients can always only understand the philosophy through the problems and experiences which derive and relate to their own world. We know that not even astonishment ("taumadzein") turns the consciousnesss of humanity into a blank page. It is always only from a particular perspective that astonishment ("taumadzein") removes "appearance" and "prejudice" from the foreground of consciousness. However, this perspective is always determined in one way or another by everyday life. Gadamer describes the core of interpretation as the "thinking mediation of past with present life"; according to the radical formula of Georg Lukács' early philosophy of art, *every interpretation is a misinterpretation*.

Philosophical systems are just as "inexhaustible" as works of art are. The possible interpretations of them are therefore also endless. One understanding can always confront another understanding, so that this — like every understanding — contains the moment of misunderstanding. "Every understanding is a misunderstanding" certainly does not mean that every misunderstanding is also an understanding. There is however nothing more difficult than to define the "boundary" beyond which a misunderstanding understanding becomes an understanding misunderstanding. This can probably only be determined in each individual case. It is possible however to lay down one basic principle which has the same validity for interpreting philosophy as it does for interpreting art. Misunderstanding ceases to be understanding when it is an interpretation which alters the value hierarchy of the system that is being interpreted. Anybody who claims that for Plato the highest good is enjoyment, or for Marx the commodity relationship, clearly completely lacks any comprehension of the material that is being interpreted, just as in the same way nobody could claim that in *Hamlet* Rosencrantz and Guildenstern are morally superior figures to Horatio. If the underlying value hierarchy of a philosophy is not received as it is, then there is no doubt that *this* philosophy is not the one that is being interpreted. If statements are ascribed to philosophers who never made them, then that is not misunderstanding, but ignorance.

The recipients of philosophy always objectify themselves: this objectification is always based on the understanding/ misunderstanding mediation between the present and the chosen philosophical system. Objectification occurs in different forms: through discussion, through correspondence, or through the publication of thoughts that have been written down. The mediation is also possible in several different forms: as application, as "hole-filling", as an apologia in response to critique or as mobilisation of new arguments in the course of the apologia.

So far the reception of philosophy has been discussed in terms of the highest type of reception, the complete reception. To this however it must be added that there is no rigid dividing line between philosophical recipients and philosophers. More precisely, it is part of the nature of philosophy that there be no rigid barrier between philosophical reception and philosophy.

Philosophical reception always in itself constitutes an active relationship to philosophy. To the extent that philosophical recipients fully experience the philosophy they have chosen, think it through to the end and misunderstandingly understand it, then they themselves also develop a philosophical orientation and see, think and behave like philosophers. Therefore, in the creation of a philosophical system, the understanding misunderstanding has a quite different function to what it has in the reception of art, or more carefully formulated, it can have a different function. Namely, it is possible that the understanding misunderstanding does not lead to a misunderstanding but to a new philosophy and to a new philosophical system. Thus, with his *Critique of Revelation* Fichte saw himself as an interpreter of Kant. That he was not, but this "misunderstanding" was not a misinterpretation but rather the beginning of the formation of a new philosophical system which differed from the Kantian one.

Today the divide between creators and recipients in the case of art is frequently questioned and bemoaned as the unfortunate consequence of the division of labour. Certainly if one considers art in its entirety the gap between artistic creators and their public has widened and deepened considerably over the last two centuries of the bourgeois world epoch. This is an expression of the fact that the creation of the beautiful has ceased to be an organic part of humanity's daily life. The dying out of the stratum of philosophical connoisseurs, as has already been pointed out, is a parallel process to this.

This negative tendency also affects, albeit at the same time in a different way, the social function of the philosophical recipient. Recipients who stand outside the discipline of philosophy can only "consume" philosophy: they are barred from any participation in its co-creation. In philosophical controversies people only get a hearing if they have already acquired a name for themselves in another area of the social division of labour. Anyone who is a prominent politician, or who is a great natural scientist or linguist, is allowed to "trespass" in the preserves of philosophy, and indeed in areas which have nothing to do with politics, the natural sciences, linguistics or whatever. "Within the trade" the restriction applies the other way round: those involved cannot for example allow themselves, as they could if they followed the normal norm of philosophical recipients, to objectify themselves solely in teaching. Instead they have to write thick volumes — and many of them — quite regardless of whether or not they feel any inner drive to do so.

We have argued that it is high time for philosophy to return to itself and freely to profess its own structure and its own laws. This also means that philosophy must do everything it can to restore the normal relationship between philosophical reception and philosophical creation and to abolish the rigidified opposition between these two poles of the division of labour. The solely philosophical reception of philosophy and the creation of a new philosophy are only two extremes: life, liveliness and activity always provided philosophy with its "trough" between these two waves. A new and grand philosophy is the crest of a wave, but it is the rest of the wave that lifts the crest towards the sky. We know that philosophy does not create the basis for its own existence, but commitment to its own uniqueness is however one moment — if only one moment — through which it can contribute to the creation of the basis for its existence.

With the *partial* reception of philosophy the three moments of the rational utopia that is proposed ("Consider how you should think, consider how you should live, consider how you should act") each fulfil their function separately and in mutual isolation. They can be isolated in this way because the preconditions of partial reception do not in any way include knowledge of the whole even of one philosophical system. The appropriation of even only a single work, or of even a part of a single work, can release the feeling of "Eureka!" — "I've got it, now I see it!" In fact philosophy can reach its recipients through mediations, and it is even possible that the recipients are guided not by one philosophy but by the (from a given perspective) same or apparently same moments of several philosophies.

When the partial reception is guided only by "Consider how you should act" then we speak of *political reception*. Politics is used here *sensu lato*: we understand as political every activity which is directly concerned with changing, altering or reforming society. Certainly not every philosophy is suited to political reception — those for which this is possible are only those whose utopia is also a social utopia. To this it must be added that the rational utopia of philosophy is usually also a social utopia. Philosophy confronts what ought to be with what is and usually makes explicit the desired or the wished-for social consequences of this confrontation. Often, as for example in Hobbes, the main work culminates in this sort of utopia. In other cases the philosophers themselves ensure the discovery of the social-utopian aspects of their systems. Plato did this in *The Republic*, Bacon in *The New Atlantis*, Spinoza in the *Tractates*, Kant in *For Perpetual Peace* and in *Religion*, Fichte in *The Autonomous Merchant State*, etc.

Anyone who claims that the political reception of philosophy occurs to a certain extent "malgré elle-même"[12] makes a mistake. The majority of philosophers precisely *intended* their works to be received politically. Doubtless this ambition has always been part of the "false consciousness" of philosophy. All philosophers are convinced that they have found the Sleeping Beauty and know what it looks like, that they also know what is the true, the good and the beautiful and what is the highest good. They have judged whatever exists by this highest standard and found it wanting. They therefore also believe that as soon as this highest good has changed from what ought to be into what is, then what is will have become what is most fundamental — the good and the true.

This particular ambition of philosophy has several variations, or one might say, several main types. According to one, the world should be judged to be good when it is ruled by philosophers, according to another, when it is ruled by philosophy, according to a third, when it is organised according to the model put forward by philosophy. In Plato's *Republic* it is clearly explained that the philosophers must rule; subsequently however in the *Laws* he merely attempts to put forward a model which should be realised. Most of the thinkers of the Enlightenment were never clear whether the world of the future would lie in the hands of a philosopher-ruler — in their terminology, in the hands of an enlightened despot — or whether they should rather hope for a future in which everyone would become a philosopher. Kant's *Perpetual Peace* is clearly a constructed "model", while his *Religion* opts instead for the generalisation of philosophy. Indeed, philosophy mostly *wants* to act as an ideology. The expression "ideology" is used here consciously. Philosophy is a rational utopia, but it very rarely knows this.[13] A utopia which does not know that it is a utopia is ideally suited to becoming an ideology when it is received politically.

The reception of philosophy as political ideology is as old as philosophy itself. As early as Plato Trasymachos is presented as a man who transformed the basic rules of Sophism into political praxis; Isocrates claimed that by rejecting the social activity of those who were political followers of Plato he had proved that Plato was unfruitful, or even "dangerous", for Athens. This type of reception however first became of world-historical importance in the eighteenth century. From then on practically every movement looked for and found its "own" philosopher.[14] It is well known that before and during the Revolution the basic political standpoint of a French politician could be known merely by which philosopher he was committed to. This hardly meant that all the politicians committed to Rousseau — with certainly a few exceptions — had in any way concerned themselves with everything that their philosophical idol had said about the origin of knowledge, let alone that a politician could fully apply the form of life he had chosen and promulgated. However, the *Social Contract* or even a few elements from the work on the tyranny of freedom were enough adequately to fulfil the function of political reception. The striking utopia from *The Fable of the Bees*, according to which the common good is achieved when everyone follows their own interests, became a truism which appeared as natural in the early liberal politics of England. This did not require comprehension or even knowledge of the drawn-out socio-political observations contained in that short verse parable. Equally, Hegel could be firstly a reactionary "state ideologist", secondly a liberal ideologue and thirdly an ideologue of rejection, even of revolution, depending on what a particular political movement took for itself from the thought-world of his philosophy, which was never understood or experienced as a whole. Even Marx, who declared war on all ideology, did not escape this fate. His philosophy too did not need to be received in its entirety to be usable as the ideology of the most diverse movements.

Here we must pause. It was claimed that for the most complete form of reception, including for its highest form, philosophical reception, every understanding is at the same time a misunderstanding. That is to say, the possibility exists that every philosophical system can be understandingly misunderstood in different ways. In what then does political — partial — reception differ from philosophical reception? Perhaps in that it is purely misunderstanding, without the slightest moment of understanding?

The situation is in fact rather different. Incidentally, in the case of political reception one can *just as little* speak of understanding as in the case of the other partial types of reception. One can only understand, and also only misunderstandingly understand, a philosophical system when all three moments are grasped together. In political reception the "Think how you should act" is separated from the other two moments, so that this form of reception cannot be described as an "understanding" of the philosophical system. And yet in this case one cannot speak of mere misunderstanding. It was certainly stated that one can and must only decide in each individual concrete case whether it is a question of a pure misunderstanding or whether more is involved. And yet we have given one clear criterion of "misunderstanding", namely that the recipient must not disrupt the value hierarchy of the philosophy. In the case of a political reception this cannot be the case, precisely because the reception is only partial. The recipient isolates a moment of the value-world of the system — the others are therefore not placed in the "wrong" position in the hierarchy, but instead simply do not exist. Ideological reception is neither understanding nor misunderstanding, but rather the "stressing" of one or more ideas, values or formulas within the whole, and indeed in relation to action, to the successful guiding of action. Who can really claim that Constantine's dream "In hoc signo vinces" was "based" on an understanding or a misunderstannding of Christianity? For ideological recipients a philosophical thought, value or idea really is a "signum", a symbol, under whose protection they gain victory, with which they confirm their victories or defeats, with which they confirm activity or abstention from activity. It is quite a different matter that ideological recipients frequently choose for themselves a philosophical type of reception, or that they prefer a particular philosophical reception of their philosophical hero to others.

The type of partial reception of philosophy in which the moment "Consider how you should live" is isolated from the other two moments, we shall term "revelatory reception". Since the reception of "how you should live" is separated from the recommendations "Consider how you should think, how you should act", the recipient to whom philosophy has been "revealed" does not intend *any generalisation* of the form of life recommended by philosophy. Philosophy is here nothing other than *a means* to give one's own life meaning or to "reveal" the meaning of one's life. In this case too, as in the case of the aesthetic reception, it is a question of a reception based on feelings. While however the aesthetic recipient arrives in the course of catharsis at a new Weltanschauung, in the case of revelation the recipient finds in the received philosophy an answer to particular questions, such as "Why am I in the world?" or "Why must this happen to me?" etc.

Not every philosophy is equally suitable for a revelatory reception. The philosophies which are especially suitable are those which focus sharply on the problem of "How should I live?" such as Stoicism, Epicureanism or the philosophy of Plotinus, yet all the same every other philosophy contains the possibility of revelatory reception.

Not every historical period is equally suited to revelatory reception. Its general occurrence has two preconditions. The first is the collapse of community. As long as one is "born into" a community in which the norms are binding for all, then the need to find an answer to these questions does not manifest itself. The second precondition is the loosening of religious *maxims*. Anyone who believes unconditionally in the divinity of Christ will, when they are alone and faced with the problems of life, turn to religion. They will not seek in a philosophy an adequate answer to the question of "Why am I in this world?"

For one of the most beautiful and one of the most authentic accounts of revelatory reception we have to thank Thomas Mann: the encounter of Thomas Buddenbrooks with Schopenhauer's philosophy. Here one sees interwoven everything that has been said about revelatory reception. The community of the hero is shattered: capitalism is well on the way to radically destroying patrician society. His belief in traditional religion is shattered: the answers that it offers are no longer relevant for him and his fate. It is at this point that his encounter with Schopenhauer occurs: reading him Thomas suddenly "understands" everything, he has the feeling that everything that the philosopher writes refers *to him*, is meant *precisely for him*. At the same time he does not understand at all a large part of the text which he is reading, and he does not want to understand it philosophically. He does not even read the work through to the end: for him what is important is not Schopenhauer's work in its entirety, but merely the moment in it which illuminates *his* life.

It clearly emerges from this that revelatory reception satisfies a religious need. Traditional religion has long lost its authority, while the religious need still exists and is even still growing. It may sound paradoxical but it is absolutely true: even atheism can satisfy the religious need. It is not unusual for the revelatory reception to lead to the insight that there is no God. The conclusion is: what has happened to me has not been done by God, so I will no longer pray to him.

When a bright light strikes our eye we do not see the source of the light. Similarly, the revelatory reception cannot be termed either understanding or misunderstanding. When somebody reads the first book of Spinoza's *Ethics* and calls out, "There is no God!" — it is just as meaningless to claim that they have misunderstood Spinoza as to claim that they have understood him.

The revelatory reception is not the reception of a particular area of knowledge. Neither history nor the history of knowledge reports it. What we know of it we know *from* art and *from* artists. Artists have often experienced a revelatory reception of philosophy and they themselves bear witness to this. And yet here one cannot speak of a reception of the knowledge of philosophy. It is extremely rare for the artist's *personal* reception of philosophy to be embodied as the *basic building block* in the *work of art*. When nonetheless this does occasionally occur — one thinks of the "presence" of Stoicism in the poems of Horace, of the presence of mystical philosophy in those of Angelus Silesius, of the presence of the Platonism of the Renaissance in the sculpture of Michelangelo — then the revelatory reception becomes more than an artistic reception and instead a reception of the knowledge of philosophy per se.

This is because the moment of the revelatory reception which satisfies the religious need is irrelevant as a principle of artistic *creation*.

The *third type* of partial reception singles out the moment "Consider how you should think" from the triple unity of the rational utopia. In this case philosophy guides neither the immediate action nor the form of life, but rather cognition. For this reason we term this type *cognition-guiding* reception. Here it is primarily a question of a reception of knowledge. Thus for example the sciences, or to be more exact, the scientists, appropriate philosophy from the stand-point of their scientific tasks.

Not every philosophy is equally suited to be the occasion for cognition-guiding reception. Its suitability depends upon the extent to which the justification of cognition is central to it. In some periods this type of reception cannot be said to occur at all, and even when the possibility for it exists, it does not always have the same importance. The cognition-guiding reception has a different status for the natural and for the social sciences. Unfortunately it is necessary to ignore here the often very important historical details and the countless differentia specifica of the different disciplines. We are quite clear that grouping together problems, which is here unavoidable, produces inaccuracies and a schematism which would have to be corrected.

If we claim that the emergence of the cognition-guiding reception is a result of the emergence of modern science we are only describing the main tendency: the successive dissolution from philosophical thought of firstly the natural and then the social sciences. This is an emancipation process which is Janus-faced. The first "face" is the delimitation of the areas of work of the different sciences, the formation of their own methodologies and so the start of their own immanent development, the creation and the realisation of the preconditions for their application. In this context we understand the emancipation of science as a *process of emancipation*.

Incidentally, modern philosophy — even if not all of it — itself justified this emancipation and strove to promote it.

Philosophy believed in this emancipation when it only existed in embryonic form; it was already behaving in this way when the path-breakers of the modern scientific world-view were themselves unclear as to their own methodological innovation. Both Copernicus and Kepler were convinced that with their new views of the universe they had justified a model and an incarnation of the "highest good" and of "perfection". Perhaps one of the reasons why Galileo, amongst others, can be considered as the real founder of modern science is that he consciously broke with philosophical preconditions: for him the category of perfection no longer had any meaning in natural science research, or in nature itself.

"The emancipation of the natural sciences" means that science no longer needed for its development any philosophical reception. This certainly does not mean that specific natural science disciplines have not now and then been recipients of the methodology of specific philosophies. Natural scientists necessarily reflect on the social relevance of their discipline, namely on where the immanent development of the natural sciences might be leading. This self-reflection is particularly important today, when it is completely clear that the pragmatic attitude to the social use and application of scientific results (an attitude which follows from the immanent nature of science) can have serious consequences for the whole of humanity. If the immanent nature of the development of the natural sciences cannot be questioned, it is all the more necessary however to question the extension of this pragmatic behaviour to the application of scientific results. Increasingly the natural scientists of today want to become philosophical recipients, because they want to know how and if scientific results can be applied and which forms of application should be preferred. They seek therefore the connection between the "true" and the "good". It is enough to refer here to the controversy between Leo Szilard and Edmund Teller over atomic experiments, or to the ever more heated controversy over the possibility of changing the genetic code. Natural scientists therefore again want to become philosophical recipients with regard to the relation between their discipline and society. However, a philosophy that was only a servant could not satisfy this need. Philosophy must have its *own* structure and its *own* truth in order to satisfy this need.

Unlike the natural sciences, in the course of their emancipation the social sciences have never ceased — nor could they ever cease — to be recipients of philosophy. In every historical period, while philosophy has denied responsibility for them, the social sciences themselves have created their own philosophers: Freud in psychology, Weber and Durkheim in sociology.[15]

At this point we must make clear that the emancipation of the social sciences is also a *factual* emancipation: the social sciences are not and cannot be identical with philosophy. They cannot afford Fichte's arrogant stance: "So much the worse for the facts." They want to understand what is, or they reconstruct it as facticity, or — in addition to this — by contrast they research the concrete possibilities inherent in empirical reality. They do not investigate what would have been a "good" legal system for ancient Rome, but rather investigate how the legal system in ancient Rome was created and how it functioned. Social science has long ago turned away from questions which refer to the "ideal". Thus aesthetics — an extremely philosophical discipline — poses questions about the "beautiful" or the canon of artistic works, for example about the connections between the artistic canon and the "spirit of the time"; the sociology of art investigates the reception of art and the nature of taste, the connections between social conflict and stylistic trends — all in a given specific historical period.

At the same time however social scientists need to receive some form of philosophy in order to be clear as to their *own* task. The mere discovery and cataloguing of social facts is an extreme case and can anyway hardly be considered as science, for no connection between the facts is constructed. Sciences become genuine sciences of society through a *social theory*, on the basis of which the facts can be placed in context and the given facts turned into the facts *of the theory*. This ordering principle always consists of two components: *method* and *value*. Method itself stems largely from philosophy, although doubtless every theoretical social science discipline possesses methods and methodological principles appropriate to its object. This does not however apply to values.

The value or values which guide the theory can stem from two sources. Firstly, social scientists can start from values that are present in their everyday life and in their everyday consciousness, values which are indeed unreflected. Such values are taken almost as "natural". In this case social scientists are guided in the production of theory by the system of prejudices of their period and social class, and of which they mostly have no consciousness at all. They can even assume that their starting point is value-neutral, since it is not guided by some value system constructed by a philosophy. However, we know that there is no such thing as "empty" consciousness, not even when philosophical astonishment ("taumadzein") has been carried out and the world is being posed "childish" questions. When not even this occurs, then every prejudice is simply transposed into the theory and appears there in a mask of apparent self-evidentness. When Max Weber demanded value neutrality in social theory, he was in his polemics quite correctly attacking this routine and unreflected value transposition. However, value freedom does not form a realistic alternative to control by the value system of unreflected everyday thought. This is not just because value freedom is unachievable: in philosophy the unachievable can still act as a guiding principle. Philosophically seen, the claim for its impossibility is not an argument against Max Weber. What is decisive is that it is not only impossible, but also *undesirable*. In our opinion the desirable alternative is the reception of the value system or value hierarchy of a philosophy and its self-conscious application in the creation of a theory. However, in so far as philosophy gives the social sciences values or a value hierarchy, and in so far as social theory absolutely consciously applies this to the theory, then we are no longer dealing merely with a reception that guides cognition, but rather with an *evaluative and cognition-guiding reception*.

Within social theory the evaluative and cognition-guiding

reception is certainly not new. Today economics is a discipline of purely instrumental rationality which accepts the everyday world as "facticity", but its origins do not lie in such limited ideas. In order to build the theoretical bases of their systems, both the physiocrats and the founders of classical English economics very consciously received the values of different philosophies: Smith and Ricardo chose as their guiding principles the theory of utility — the *utopia* of the self-regulating market — and the anthropology of bourgeois philosophy. This is no less true if Smith, who himself was also a philosopher, was more conscious of doing this than Ricardo, who was in fact only a partial recipient of philosophy. This type of reception is completely ignored by the scorn of the positivist social sciences, but in a more contemporary perspective the existence of schools of historiography influenced by Hegel, Marx, Dilthey, Gadamer, Wittgenstein and others is enough to indicate that it has never been completely rooted out.

To repeat: even evaluative and cognition-guiding reception is a partial reception in that it stresses the moment "Consider how you should think". Here the construction of theory takes place through the application of certain guiding values of the philosophy, but since these values only guide *cognition*, this does not make it in any way a route to complete reception. Several of Marx's methodological principles and even guiding values have "gone over" into individual social sciences, but this has hardly made their representatives socialists, let alone made them understand themselves as Marxists.

There are several reasons why the social sciences are evaluative and cognition-guiding recipients of philosophy. Firstly, this doubtless involves them in a step towards de-fetishisation in social theory: the abstraction from the system of prejudices of everyday consciousness. This creates room in social theory for the moment of "taumadzein" — the questioning of whatever appears to be self-evident. Secondly, the conscious choice of values and the commitment to these values makes possible a value discussion between theoretical systems. Hence the hurdles of everyday value discussions can at least be avoided. And thirdly, an evaluative and cognition-guiding reception *can* prepare the way for a *complete* reception of philosophies. This however is *one* precondition for the coming together again of philosophy and social theory. Such an encounter does not mean a "unity", for neither of the two can give up its *own* structure. Yet they can *mutually engage each other for a mutual task*. In the third part of this study we will consider this problem from the point of view of philosophy.

CONCLUSION

There is one further question that has to be considered in a discussion of the different types of philosophical reception. It results from the fact which we have already noticed that each of the different types of recipient has a *different and specific need for philosophy*.

The analysis of the complete reception of philosophy showed that the *polis* of Athens can serve as a model for this type; subsequently there followed the seventeenth century and finally the century of philosophy — excluding classical German philosophy *up to* the French Revolution. The nearer we come to the present, the more problematic this type becomes. We were forced to recognise that the connoisseur as a recipient of philosophy probably no longer exists: genuinely philosophical reception has become ever more problematic. Philosophers — great philosophers, important philosophers — are no longer the "crest" of a wave, they no longer emerge from amongst a community of creators and fellow-thinkers. Instead they have become slaves to the division of labour and have to force their way to the new despite the "job".

When however we came to the partial type of reception the situation was suddenly the other way round. We found that although partial types of reception had existed earlier (though this was incidentally not true in the case of the cognition-guiding type of reception), the "grande époque" of political reception *began* with the French Revolution and cognition-guiding reception in the social sciences also dates from approximately this period. Although inspirational reception has indeed always existed, it experienced its heyday in the period when the normative system of the community and the belief in inherited religion were decaying. Hence precisely the modern period is the most fertile soil for religious need, for religious atheism and so for the revelatory reception of philosophy.

There can be no doubt about it. Both the mounting difficulties facing a complete reception of philosophy and the generalisation and multiplication of the types of partial reception are *manifestations of one and the same process*. The need for the partial reception of philosophy *is the expression and manifestation of the need for philosophy in a period in which its complete reception has become more and more difficult*. It was pointed out earlier that one of the factors that has caused this process is the division of labour between the different "jobs": politics and the exercise of the different scientific disciplines have become specialised "careers". Yet by itself this is no explanation. We could conclude that the appropriation of a profession, the "engagement" with it and the accumulation of tasks or of scientific material now all make it impossible for anyone who is so "overloaded" with learning or other tasks to concern themselves in detail with philosophy. Yet if we did this, we would have to take back everything we have said so far about philosophy. It is in no way a precondition for philosophical thinking, for the appropriation and complete reception of a philosophical system, that individuals accumulate a new and differently constructed knowledge "beyond" or "in addition to" their existing knowledge. Rather the sole precondition is that people categorise and think through from the perspective of the good and the true of a rational utopia everything that they already know, experience and undergo. If we claim that people have "no time" for philosophy, we do not therefore solve the problem. Not only is this no answer: it is a misleading pseudo-answer.

In fact the root of the evil should not be sought in the piling up of partial knowledges, but rather in the social context in which these specialised disciplines function. The *connection* between the *partial* and the *general* is dissolved, and in two ways. Partial knowledge — as discipline and as occupation —

atrophies more and more into a function which is opposed to the other functions of the individual: the unity of the personality thus dissolves into different roles. Even before the emergence of the world epoch of bourgeois society, philosophy suspected that the division of labour amongst the disciplines would have this grave consequence: it suffices to recall Rousseau or Ferguson. At the same time a discipline that is a partial discipline cannot provide a starting point for confrontation *with the problems of society in their entirety*: the whole — in so far as it exists for consciousness — only exists *from the point of view* of the partial. Wherever the individual dissolves into "roles", knowledge cannot be a form of life, and action occludes questions which concern *the preconditions of action*. Where no road leads from the partial to the all-inclusive universal, questions such as "How shall I live?" and "What is the meaning of life?" are always *private questions*.

However, the split between the part and the whole is only a tendency, although one that is becoming ever stronger, and it directly produces counter-tendencies. The partial reception of philosophy is itself an expression of this counter-tendency. It is the expression of the need somehow or other and despite everything to relate the partial to the whole, and to create out of the chaos of parts a cosmos: either the cosmos of a unitary world-view or the cosmos of a unitary personality. One or other cosmos, but not both: philosophical reception can only structure the relation of the part to the whole from both aspects if it is already a complete reception, that is to say, if the moments of "How should one think", "How should one act" and "How should one live" are not isolated from each other.

As we know, philosophy is a rational utopia. It orders what is according to the measure of what should be in terms of the good and the true. It constructs its good and true, its highest value. This highest value is called upon to guide human beings: how they should think, how they should act, how they should live. The utopia of philosophy is a utopia of value rationality and not of purposive rationality. Purposive rationality contains no utopia. Even if we define the world of pure instrumental rationality as a value, then we do not reach any utopia of instrumental rationality, but rather one of value rationality. Considered in general, the function of philosophy consists in the satisfaction of the need for value rationality.

If we consider more closely what has been said of the definition of pure purposive rationality as a value, then we see that today the constitution of pure purposive rationality as a utopian model cannot take away the purpose of philosophy: it is not philosophy, but ideology. Indeed, the highest value of philosophy is not simply any value, but rather a value which, however it varies in other respects, always has the function of de-fetishising whatever exists. The generalisation of purposive rationality produces however a value which precisely accepts complete fetishism. Thus, we can now go further and define the function of philosophy as the satisfying of the need for an unprejudiced value rationality. This too must be specified further.

It is immediately apparent that it is not only philosophy that fulfils this function, for art also does. It is no accident that in the case of one type of partial reception, namely revelatory reception, art and philosophy *can* be functionally equivalent. Philosophy however satisfies the need for a demystified value rationality from the point of view of *a form of life* which it constitutes and affirms and in the light of which it criticises the inadequacy of being. This need however it alone can fulfil. Therefore as far as the guidance of cognition and the guidance of evaluative cognition — as partial reception — are concerned, philosophy has not and cannot have any other functional equivalent in any other species-specific objectification. Nothing is further from our intention than to erect a hierarchy of the spheres of the "absolute spirit"; innumerable needs can be listed which can be satisfied by art, but not by philosophy. Our task however was to specify precisely the need for philosophy.

Yet there is a catch in everything that has been said so far. It was claimed that Kant had spoken the "secret" of all philosophies when he spoke of the primacy of practical reason. But here we appear to understand *autonomous cognition* as the characteristic single determining moment of all the functions of philosophy.

This is however no contradiction. The primacy of practical reason in philosophy means that the system is always commensurate with the highest good, with the proffered value and with the form of life. Yet we know that for philosophy the highest good is not simply true knowledge, but rather a knowledge the truth of which can only be understood through autonomous rational thought and which can only be confirmed by rational arguments. Philosophy therefore satisfies the need for a rational creation of value rationality and the need to "apply" this in autonomous thought. In philosophy there is no separation between theory and practice: *theory and practice are always fused*.

It is for this reason that we can claim that an authentic need for philosophy is only satisfied by a complete reception of philosophy. Or, to put it the other way round, the need for complete reception of philosophy is the totality of need for philosophy: it is the need to live thought.

The world of myths is gone. The fact that science has taken the place of myths and emphasis on true knowledge that of belief, that there is no longer any "credo quia absurdum", all this we regard not as degradation but as an achievement of the human spirit. The fact that in the bourgeois world epoch the growth of knowledge itself became a fetish and that the totality collapsed into incoherent "jobs" does not lead us to the conclusion that one should return to myths or to revelation. Rather we are claiming that philosophy as a rational utopia based on autonomous, rational thought, as unity of theory and practice, as a "world", is suited to *mediate* between the totality and the partial. Not because it is the science of sciences, not because it formulates "the most general laws", but because it offers us values and a form of life which allows us to live our own thoughts and to transform them into social action. If one wishes to understand the world as a whole and to understand one's own place in it as a *unitary personality*, then one needs a philosophy. The need for philosophy grows and grows: only philosophy itself does not yet know this.

In so far as we have discovered that philosophy satisfies a need, have also specified what sort of need it satisfies and have

discovered that this need is growing, we have not yet confirmed philosophy. According to these criteria philosophy
could be still a mere chimera. The need that is directed to it
must itself be confirmed.

3

Philosophy and
Everyday Experience

Philosophy constitutes the good and the true and the unity of them both into the highest good. Up to now we have considered this process from the inside, that is to say, from the point of view of the world of philosophy and its reception. If however we wish to consider critically the need that itself is directed to philosophy, then we have to start from the life process of society, which is *not* to say that this is also the object of the discussion that follows. As before, our object is philosophy, but now from the point of view of the process of social life.

We are not therefore asking whether the good or the true exist, for this question would place us inside philosophy. To claim that the good or the true do not exist is just as much an answer internal to philosophy as it is to claim that they do exist. The question now is rather whether from the standpoint of the process of social life it has any sense or any meaning to pose the question of the existence of the good and the true. And if one — if we — come to a positive answer, then we have to ask *what* sense or *what* meaning this has in relation to the process of social life.

True and false, good and bad, beautiful and ugly, all are *value orientation categories*. Value orientation belongs to our social nature, to our human existence. One can just as little "get behind" them or "transcend" them as one can everyday speech. However one thinks and acts, however one feels and experiences, we think, act, feel and experience through them. Only if we placed ourselves in a position outside society could these categories be pure objects of our thought. If I claim or deny, demand, forbid or order, love or hate, desire or detest, if I want to achieve something or to avoid something, if I laugh, cry, work, rest, judge or have twinges of conscience, then always I am guided by one or other value orientation category, indeed often by more than one. Nothing is therefore more self-evident than that every value orientation category is a *concept of everyday speech*. And it is equally self-evident that *everyone also knows* what these concepts *mean* and therefore uses them in a relevant way.

The most general pair of value orientation categories is good/bad. This pair can reasonably replace all the other pairs of value orientation categories, and therefore counts as the primary one. The following are secondary pairs: true/false, good/evil, beautiful/ugly, right/wrong, useful/harmful, successful/unsuccessful, pleasant/unpleasant, holy/profane. These usually cannot sensibly replace one another, even if several pairs are applied to the same action, thought or feeling. An action can be both beautiful and useful, yet these two concepts express two different contents. The circumstance that in exceptional cases they can be used analogously is a special problem that we do not wish to discuss here.

We talk of categories of value *orientation*, for they do actually influence all our social activities; they orientate us towards what is compulsory and what is prohibited, what is to be chosen and what is to be avoided. They are categories of *value* orientation, for only through them and with them can a social objectification system become an objectification system, that is, a *scale of values*. The value orientations are "given" in the social objectification system. If nothing were good or bad, then there would be no system of rules and therefore no society. The system of rules determines simultaneously what is the good, the pleasant, the right, etc., and indeed from the point of view of thought just as from that of the most heterogeneous types of activities. At the same time it also provides the hierarchy of values. What is labelled as holy stands higher on the scale than that that is labelled pleasant. What is holy must be placed higher than what is pleasant, but it is advisable to prefer the pleasant to the unpleasant — so long as it does not clash with the activities that stand higher than it in the hierarchy.

The value orientation categories function as final and therefore unquestionable theoretical and practical ideas, as the incorporation of what in everyday life is the unchallengeable unity of cognition and action. This can be seen easily when one considers how human beings develop into independent social beings. In their environment humans experience the world as something that is "ordered" by value orientation categories. If one says "Don't do that, that is bad", then the world of their experience is enriched in that the thing that has been named has been classified in their developing understanding under the category "bad" and "to be avoided". At the same time they receive a norm in relation to action: that is something one must not do, that is a way one should not act.

The different value orientation categories guide human behaviour, thought and feeling in different ways. It should be added that in any attempt to grasp these different aspects one immediately sees that the value orientations are never "pure". They only appear in comparatively pure form when the species-specific objectifications for themselves and in and for themselves become abstracted from the objectifications in themselves. We can accurately speak of such a differentiation from the beginning of the civilised epoch. From then up to the present day, however, everyday life is and remains the basis of our knowledge, of our behaviour and of our world of feelings. The language of philosophy, science and literature must never and can never abstract completely from ordinary language and must be always able to return to it. Therefore this "purity" can only be relative.

Despite all such relativity however, we can attempt to trace out the areas to which the different value orientation categories apply. The pair of orientation categories true/false governs knowledge, good/evil governs morality, right/wrong the following of rules in general, successful/unsuccessful the achievement of concrete objectives or the selection of means (for example in work), beautiful/ugly the sphere of spiritual enjoyment, useful/harmful the economy and the socially determined satisfaction of the needs of our organism.

All the same, if anyone desires complete conceptual clarity here, they will become confused in relation to all the value orientation categories, and this for several reasons. To name the simplest: for every value orientation category there exists one use that is *adequate to the object*, one that is *adequate to the subject* and one that is *adequate to the situation*. One can therefore use it "applied to the thing" or "the task", "applied to the situation" or "applied to the person". One can say of anyone that they are "beautiful", but one can also say, "For me you are beautiful": the orientation category "beautiful" is relevant in both contexts. In his history of art Gombrich frequently warns against judging a fresco on the basis of a reproduction: the fresco is only beautiful in its place and in its function in the church. Because Aristotle formulated a substantive value ethic, it appeared to him self-evident that this threefold division also applied to the good, for it was not simply a question of practising virtue in action, but also of applying it in a correct manner and finding a correct "means" in one's own world of feelings. Already therefore the positivist concept of "true" has to be questioned, because it cannot define a use of the concept "true" that is adequate to the subject, as for example in the formulation "a true feeling".

It appears equally self-evident (though it is not so to everyone) that in different historical periods the different value orientation categories have been applied in completely different spheres, systems of objectification, types of activity, etc. It is thus possible for the pair of categories beautiful/ugly to be only applied to people, while a work of art can count not as "beautiful" but as "holy".

It has already been mentioned that the value orientation categories function as theoretical and practical ideals. This creates the possibility that they can be applied to spheres to which they cannot be applied from within the objectification system of our society. However small or wide the divergence may be, such divergences can lead to values being slowly reformulated. However, this sort of modification is probably only possible within *dynamic* social structures: in ancient Egypt it was not possible even for a pharaoh.

We have linked the construction of relatively "pure" value orientation categories (the differentiation of which category is to be applied to which situation) to the uncoupling of the species-specific objectifications for-themselves and in- and for-themselves from the world of objectifications in-themselves; by contrast the normal use of value orientation categories as relatively *"free" ideas* has been linked to the emergence of dynamic societies. Use as "free ideas" means that it is possible to formulate, express and practise a *concrete application* of value orientation categories in society both in relation to the spheres in which they are applied and in relation to the *criteria* by which they are applied. The Athenian polis was such a dynamic society. I have discussed elsewhere the circumstance that precisely this dynamism brought about the collapse of the polis.[16]

We need also to mention, if only in passing, that a religion such as the Judaeo-Christian religion is also to be thanked for the use of value orientations as free ideas. Jerusalem too was a dynamic polis society and hence fitted consciously to question the old inherited values and to be able to apply value orientation categories in a fully new fashion. The common source of monotheism and philosophical questioning leaps to the eye. As long as it is impossible to articulate and to practise that not this but that is true, that not this but that is beautiful, that not this but that is good, then it is impossible to pose the question as what is the truth, the real truth, the only truth, the eternal truth, and what is the good, the highest good, the eternal and everlasting good. Yet to these questions monotheism gives a transcendental answer: there is one good and one truth, there is a unity of the good and the true — the eternal, single, true God. Because this answer is transcendental, it cannot be questioned any further. It is common knowledge that historical changes in the use of value orientations have "shaped" God himself and humanity's relationship to him. It is however impossible to go beyond this and ask what is the highest good and the highest truth without renouncing religion itself, for that too is a collective understanding and not a free and rational utopia of an individual.

Philosophy is the *independent creation of the dynamic Greek polis*, above all of Athens. Yet there also cannot be any doubt that statements such as "Not this but that is good", "Not this but that is beautiful" — in other words, the "free" use of value orientation categories — were the precondition for the actual ability to pose questions about the good and the true as such.

Philosophy therefore did not develop the philosophical ideas of "the true", "the good" and "the beautiful" by questioning the *nature* of value orientation categories. Philosophy's fundamental ideas arose far more as the *generalisation of value judgements*. Philosophy develops its ideas of the good, the beautiful and the true from the value judgements "Not this but that is good", "Not this but that is true" and "Not this but that is beautiful". Philosophical ideas are therefore always a criticism of every use and every application of the value orientation categories which contradict the claim formulated in the idea. One can see in almost all philosophers what particular value judgements they have generalised into an idea. In his *Republic* Plato opposes the arguments of Trasymachos with the value judgement that it is better to suffer injustice than to commit it, and from this value he constitutes the highest good. The question "What does 'good' mean?" or "What is 'good'?" certainly cannot be answered, but it refers to everyday experience. A philosophical idea is therefore always a viewpoint; only thus can it also be utopian. When the value judgement "This is not good, but that is good" is elevated to an idea it means at the same time that, in contradiction to the current view, that *should* be good.

Since in the history of dynamic societies the application of the value orientation categories is continually changing (in terms of both the sphere in which they are applied and the criteria by which they are applied), the generalisation of value judgements into ideas must also be changing. This has to happen if only for the reason that in a given period the phrase "This is not good" always criticises whatever is the usual general application of the characterisation "good". Equally, the phrase "But that is good" only has any meaning when it is confronted with what is being criticised. Every new philosophy therefore expresses a new "Not this but that is good" and generalises it into an idea. If however, in a given period, on the basis of different value judgements two philosophers question the current understanding of the value orientations, then the one will say, "Not this but that is true", while the other will claim, "Not that but this is true", and the generalisation of these claims into an idea will follow the two value judgements: two philosophical ideas of the good will confront each other. The concepts of true, good, and beautiful in the different philosophies are as numerous as the value judgements from which they have been generalised into ideals. The value judgements which serve as starting points determine the particular *meaning and content* of these ideas.

The fact that every philosophy — or at least the overwhelming majority of philosophies — recognises only its own ideas as good and true initially merely means that it is claiming universal validity for these values. This claim however cannot be questioned. Every value which understands itself to be true has to raise this claim to universal validity. The problem lies in the fact that philosophy has not reflected on the historical preconditions of its own ideas. This was not a problem before the emergence of modern historical consciousness, but since its appearance the status of philosophy has become more and more questionable. From this point on, philosophy faces the task of *reflecting on itself as historically determined and simultaneously upholding the claim that its ideas are universally valid* — and into the bargain *proving* that this claim is justified. Later I wish to sketch a possible solution to this problem, but before that numerous questions still have to be resolved.

Above all we have to find an answer to the question why philosophy generalises precisely that value judgement which it has developed with the help of the value orientation categories good, true and beautiful. Why for example is the application of value orientation categories such as pleasant, useful or holy not the basis of judgement?

Humans recognise binding and non-binding value orientation categories. Binding value orientation categories are those which demand from people that they rise above particularity; non-binding ones are those which do not make such a demand. Only the moral orientation category, the good, and the cognition-guiding category, the true, have clear binding functions. All the other categories are only binding if they contain a moral aspect. This applies to the "holy" in all religions in which the relationship to the transcendental possesses a moral value content, and to the "beautiful" in societies where the category either has or aims to have a moral or religio-moral content. Following the particular value orientation category that is internal to an activity also involves a binding aspect, because this also contains a moral aspect. Thus in the end it is also a moral question whether or not someone successfully carries out work with which they have been entrusted, or whether or not scientists always check if their claims are true. In the spectrum of binding and non-binding the other extreme is undoubtedly the pleasant. The orientation to the pleasant is always non-binding and is never binding.

It is therefore *not* philosophy which creates the hierarchy of value orientation categories. No society, however "primitive", is known in which this hierarchy does not exist. To the extent that philosophy stresses the good and the true, it merely canonises the de facto, already existing hierarchy of value judgements. Philosophy therefore generalises its fundamental idea not through any value judgements, but rather always through those which are socially categorised, applied and experienced as the highest types of value judgements.

Something however must be added to this. Philosophy only rarely excludes from its system the non-binding value orientation categories; it merely places them below the good, thus confirming the hierarchy of value orientations that exists at the time. Even Plato includes in the good the pleasant as a subordinate moment. Aristotle does not doubt for a moment that usefulness, success and pleasantness are values, and he grants them a place, if at the same time one that is subordinate to virtue, in the empire of the highest good. The divorce of the binding from the non-binding, and even more, the confrontation of the one with the other, occurs in sentimental philosophy with Kant's categorical imperative for the first time in the history of philosophy.

It is certainly no novelty to claim that Kant's conception is also a philosophical generalisation of "Not this but that is good". Equally, there is nothing new in understanding which need created this radicalism of sentimental philosophy precisely from the standpoint of the social functions of value orientation categories. When naive philosophy declared that not "this" was good but "that", it constructed its highest good in such a way that it always referred to *existing values*. It chose one method of applying the value orientation categories, confronted it with another, expanded its usage, gave a new content to it or added a broader one, in order then to declare: "Look at the good, this is the highest good!" Up until Kant bourgeois philosophy by and large followed the same path. In the ever more property-orientated bourgeois world it shifted the value hierarchy in favour of the *useful* and the *successful*. More and more everyday thought identified the useful with the good and the non-binding value orientation category thus absorbed the binding category within itself. In this way naive philosophy, of whatever form, was expressing an existing social process, namely the transformation of moral judgement. It in no way abandoned the good as the highest good, but rather was concerned to deduce the good itself from the useful. Kant however wanted to turn his back completely on the bourgeois use of value orientation categories: therefore he could *in no way accept the conventional value judgements*. In order to be able to recreate an imperative and binding form of morality this imperative had to be *categorical*: it could no longer be based on non-bindingness or on accident, but had to reject them. Countless philosophical problems and antinomies resulted from this, but we have no space to discuss them here.

Deducing the good from the useful is a very characteristic example of a hopeless philosophical task. Value orientation categories form the ordering principle of our thought, behaviour and action, and constitute our social nature precisely by their *heterogeneity*. Equally, just as one cannot "go behind" them and think or do something without them, so one cannot deduce one category from the others. It is self-evident that in certain historical periods two heterogeneous orientation categories are or can be assigned to the same thing or the same action. Since Max Weber we have all known that in early Protestantism large property and social success were considered as confirmation of "virtue" or as virtue itself. As soon as this judgement is expressed in a philosophical idea, then the value judgement that property is the fruit of virtue takes on the appearance of a mutual relationship between the good and the useful. Various experiences and ideologies, which are diffuse but nonetheless all lead in the same direction, find their formulation sub specie aeternitatis:[17] *the good can be deduced from the useful.* We owe this belief to those mental gymnastics according to which altruism and self-sacrifice are "really" egoism, indeed, that they represent *real* egoism. As soon as one attempts to deduce one value orientation category from another, *it loses its meaning* and this is so even in normal everyday speech. It makes no difference if "useful" here is understood not as useful to the individual, but as "useful" to a collective entity or to the integration of a group.

The fact that one value orientation category cannot be deduced from another does not mean that two categories cannot be linked to each other. They can be linked in human striving and activity. The beautiful, the good and the true are always generalisations of value judgements. Yet the generalisation of value judgements into one idea or into several interconnected ideas always has a guarantee: the person who strives equally for the good, the true and the beautiful. Without such a "guarantee" the idea of connection could not even have occurred. The "guarantee" of Greek philosophy is the person who incorporates this connection.

But does this guarantee offer any real security? To play on one of Marx's expressions, value orientation categories are the Moloch in us all. They existed, exist and will exist, and for us all. Everything to which they can be applied enters into a "value relationship" and becomes a value upon which a value judgement can be passed. Are we, however, led and controlled in our acts, in our forms of behaviour and in our thinking by the generalisations of value judgements into "the good", the "beautiful" and "the true", by the ideas which the philosophical tradition characterises as "ideals"?

Does any person whatsoever exist who strives for "the" good, "the" true, "the" beautiful, and hence for the ideals? Do we not have in front of us here a philosophical monstrosity? When someone thinks about a problem, they are hardly searching for "the true" — they want to solve the problem. When someone reads a book and finds a convincing solution, they will say "That is true", but not "That is the true". If a person wants to compose a sonata, they want to create something beautiful, but who would want to compose "the beautiful"? One may excitedly clap one's hands together and exclaim, "Isn't the sunset beautiful?" but who would say "Isn't that the beautiful?" People wish to follow customary norms, stand the test of moral conflicts, develop in themselves an ability to sympathise and to be tactful, but they do not strive after "the good". Nobody would be confused if they heard the phrase "I want to be good". "Good" here is not the same as "the good"; it is largely a synonym for "kindhearted", and, with a child, for "wellbehaved" or "obedient". Nobody strives after the ideal. Only in philosophy and in some religions do "the good", "the beautiful" and "the true" exist.

Philosophy however does not generalise value orientation categories, but rather develops concrete value judgements into ideals. This has both a structural and a substantive aspect. The structural aspect is that philosophy often brings *together* in their mutual relationships and contexts the good, the true and frequently also the beautiful. These therefore relate not to the person who seeks the beautiful, the good or the true, but to the person who searches for the true in *all* good, the good in *all* true, and in *both* the beautiful. We will see later whether such a person or such a search exists from whose standpoint this structure is relevant.

The substantive aspect is that the generality of the philosophical ideal is, as Hegel would say, a *concrete generality*.[18] That however means that philosophy always "unfolds" its ideals. On the one hand it "translates" them into the language of concrete value judgements or into descriptions and theories controlled by values, on the other hand it recommends *how* a person can act according to these values. The ideal thus concretises itself so that it gives an answer to questions of how one should live and act; it offers a concrete form of life. To define an ideal is always to summarise *specific meanings*: the ideal of philosophy is *factually* therefore the general that is concrete. If philosophical ideals started from the orientation categories themselves, they would not be the generalisation of a concrete application of particular orientation categories, but rather an attempt to generalise the orientation categories themselves. Then not only would philosophy be pointless, but also its ideals could not be any concrete general ideas.

We now wish to consider briefly three problems. First, do all philosophies' ideals of the good and the true, or their ascent to them and to their implications, have a common basis?[19] Second, how and in what way is a specific period of historical development shaped by its philosophies and ideals? What criteria determine these? Third, who is the real guarantor of philosophy?

In every philosophy true *knowledge* is the true as opposed to mere opinion or mere prejudice. The true guides us in cognition and in action; it is the *reliable* guide to both. We accept responsibility for the true: true knowledge is *conviction*. True knowledge includes our knowledge *of the world* and our knowledge of *ourselves*. One should strive after true knowledge. The search for true knowledge is a theoretical orientation which demands the transcendence of our particularity. Everybody can acquire true knowledge, if they systematically use their good sense and their reason.

The "truth" of philosophy therefore cannot be abstracted from the good: it always contains a moral aspect. This applies even to Kant, who certainly separated the true, the good and the beautiful, but in order to link them with the help of "ideas" or by the mediation of the power of judgement. Indeed in his philosophy of history he goes further and makes this unity explicit.

In philosophy the good is not necessarily *morality itself*. In any case the good is a value which is either the *precondition* for morality or at least present as a component of it. Every philosophy knows a highest good to which it relates all the other values, even when it does not actually use this concept. The fact that the highest good is a value can be understood by every reasonable being. In philosophy the highest good is therefore always *true*. As the highest placed value it guides our action and our cognition and we take upon ourselves responsibility for it. The true value *should* be realised, and in *the practical orientation* we must give up our particularity in so far as it stands in the way of this.

The good of philosophy therefore cannot be abstracted from the true of philosophy. The highest good must be true. It must guide us with certainty and reliability, *either* in cognition itself, or at least in understanding *the human world* and in judging people.

What however does it mean that somebody — both in their theoretical and in their customary practical orientation — should transcend their own particularity? To whom does this ideal refer? Is it not perhaps *the ideal of the person who has reached the level of the species*? Does not philosophy show to everyone the ideal of elevating themselves to the level of the species? Is it not precisely for this reason therefore the democratic utopia? And is it not therefore perhaps indispensable?

On the other hand is not the posing of the ideal of the true as a moral idea, the posing of the ideal of the good as truth, not *the ideal of the unity of theory and praxis*? We know that in everyday life there still is no difference between theory and praxis. However, in parallel with the continual development of the division of labour, our institutions and our objectification systems based on everyday life and thought — this basis of our knowledge and of our entire social activity — "split" human activity more and more. Certainly this splitting is productive and useful. Is it not however the function of philosophy to pose unity as an *ideal*? For this reason is not every philosophy democratic and utopian at the same time? And is philosophy not for this reason indispensable?

Such questions are not really meant seriously, for they all too easily assume a positive answer. And yet they should be taken seriously. We know that the concrete and general ideals of the various philosophies question the use of value orientation categories customary in a given historical period. Philosophy does not stand outside history; its aim and its utopia are related to the historical present. *From the standpoint of this present* it is a utopia. Does this fact make irrelevant those claims that were posed as questions?

We consider incidentally that the two claims are not mutually exclusive. This naturally should not be taken to mean that no philosophy could exist which by its concrete historicity excluded the call for the elevation to the level of the species. That would merely mean that the two moments in the ideal of philosophy can only be conceptualised together and inseparable from each other. From the beginning we have been concerned to determine clearly the ideal of philosophy. Everything that has been said up to now about philosophy however assumes a unity of the historical and the species-related.

The ideal of every philosophy is a concrete generality, and we must therefore also reflect on this historically. Since we live in a period of world-historical consciousness, we must *also reflect historically on our own ideals*. We must be conscious that our rational utopia is a utopia *of our time*. Yet the claim that the structure of philosophy — of each and every philosophy — expresses the structure of the personality which raises itself to the standpoint of the species is not contradicted by the historicity of the form of the ideals. The linkage of the good and the true corresponds both to the demand that each individual should through transcendence of their own particularity strive for the simultaneous realisation of the good and the true, and to the demand that each individual should shape their life, their action and their thought according to this norm. In its relation to the existing values of the species, philosophy expresses the structure of the developing personality independent of those aspects of development it concretely ascribes to the species-being. The fact that philosophy can only express this because the species itself develops historically and through historical conflicts is a problem which space does not allow us to discuss here.[20]

It has been said that the relationship of philosophy to the species-being is independent of those elements of development the different philosophies ascribe to the species-being. This claim must also be concretised. Namely the concretisation of the ideals, above all of the leading ideal (the highest good) is a process with several stages. Initially every philosophy defines *what* this highest good should be and therefore what value it understands as the fundamental value; it then explains what it *understands* by this fundamental value and applies it accordingly within the system of value judgements and in theoretical understandings of the world. As far as the first stage is concerned, namely the characterisation of the fundamental value as the highest good, on this all the philosophies of a world epoch would agree. It is the consensus of all philosophies of a given world epoch. The distinctiveness of the value judgements and of the ideals of the individual philosophers is revealed in the second stage, namely *how* they interpret this fundamental value and how they apply it.

In addition, all philosophies of all periods agree on two characteristics of the human being. First and above all, humans are rational thinking beings. If the philosophies did not assume this, then they would not be philosophies. Second, what is unique to humans is their ability to *value rational action*. If they did not assume this, then they equally would not be philosophies. In no way do all philosophies assume that de facto people think rationally and act according to value rationality, but they do assume that humans can only correspond to the ideal of humanity if they think rationally and act according to value rationality. In its *structure* philosophy therefore can only represent the ascent of the species because it is always convinced of these two characteristics of the human being.

It is important to be clear on this so that one does not hold philosophy's choice of ideals to be arbitrary. A choice of values which always recognises at least two characteristics of human beings as always the same cannot be completely arbitrary. A choice of values can equally hardly be completely arbitrary if within a world historical period it is always characterised by a consensus about the fundamental value of the highest good. We will now examine this second question somewhat more closely.

If one compares the two great "philosophical" periods, namely the period of classical antiquity and the bourgeois period, it is immediately clear that for classical philosophy the highest good is *happiness*, and that for bourgeois philosophy it is *freedom*. Within each particular period there was always a consensus on this. Naturally the value "freedom" was also present within the highest good of antiquity, just as the value "happiness" exists within the highest good of the bourgeois world epoch's philosophy. Even Kant defined the "highest worldly good" as a unity of freedom and happiness, yet for him, as for everyone in this epoch, freedom counted as the most highly placed value. The consensus indicates the highest good, but the interpretations of it can not only differ but can also be mutually exclusive, since the forms of life which they recommend can also be diametrically opposed to each other. In a period in which the communal ways of life are decaying, which is characterised by a hitherto unknown generalisation and expansion of the social division of labour and by a permanent struggle of the classes against each other, the ethical norms become more loose and open to choice.

And what does the philosophy of our time *say* about *our* time? If one considers the positivist philosophies which are rooted in the nineteenth century and which today are still flourishing and in a certain sense even dominant, then one could say judgement has been passed on this period. *It has been passed, in that no judgement was passed.* That is to say, positivism in all its shapes and forms *tore away from all philosophies their crown — the highest good*. There is in this philosophy no longer any highest good, and hence there can be no rational utopia. It offers no Ought to set against what is; it recommends no new or alternative forms of life. It thus, whether it wants to or not, confirms and consolidates precisely what is.

If one considers the status in this philosophy of the three leading ideals, the good, the beautiful and the true, the result is more than sad. With a brave gesture Kant's sentimental philosophy restored the beautiful to the pantheon of philosophical ideals, but now it is to be found there no longer. The beautiful is no longer the "concern" of philosophy, not even of the philosophy of art, but instead is degraded to being merely the "private concern" of artists and connoisseurs. Yet, as has already been said, in this heaven the beautiful is no dispensable god; in any case its empty place suggests a certain "emptiness" on earth. Without the highest good however this heaven does not exist at all. And yet philosophical relevance has equally been denied to the highest good — and with it to morality. It is claimed that our value judgements cannot be true and that our choice of values is "irrational" and subjective. Nothing is more revealing than the naive self-evidentness with this claim is expressed. If there is anything which can destroy ethics, it is meta-ethics. To reduce the philosophy of morality to an analysis of the logic of moral claims is "merely" to make incidental what that philosophy should express: morality itself.

The idea of the true appears to fare better. Science, the decisive productive force in the world of today, cannot do without a clear criterion of true knowledge. The fact that the ever more powerful natural sciences require a particular application and definition of the idea of true knowledge for this sphere is self-evident, and no one can doubt the right, even the duty, of philosophy to work out in this sphere the relevant idea of the true and its criteria. Yet neither science nor mathematics demands that philosophy should take the real or claimed criteria of true knowledge of their areas as a universally valid idea of truth. A philosophy which has occluded the question of the highest good and the question of the truth of values as "myths" has made science itself into a *myth*. Now neither natural science nor mathematics is an ideology. Yet all the same Habermas is correct: they *were made* into ideology. Philosophy raised them to ideology, in that it reduced the criterion of truth to logical thinking and the true knowledge of facts.

This reduction is, we must repeat, of an ideological sort. For here, as in every ideology, an individual case is generalised: the pragmatic of the natural sciences is made a criterion of all true cognition, according to which only what is quantifiable is true, and hence scientific. As such, only the quantifiable social sciences could raise a claim to truth. Every ideal, above all the ideal of the good, would thus be "unscientific", so that the truth would be irrelevant since it is precisely not quantifiable. A mathematical model is realisable and thus is scientific; the values of a utopia are unquantifiable and thus unrealisable, misleading, "unscientific". Facts, so it is claimed, are independent of values. "Practical reason", hence the ideal of the good and of morality, is out of date for theory construction and orientation to values is a "holistic myth": utopia is a term of abuse.

The widespread dissemination of this form of thinking is certainly novel, although we know from Kant that it is not completely new. In order to avoid the impression that I am befuddled by my personal prejudices, let me quote how Kant answered the precursors of positivism. Of those who opposed theory based on the ideals of duty and morality he wrote:

> To the scandal of philosophy it is often pretended that what in itself is right is nonetheless invalid in practice. This is put forward in a haughty, disdainful tone which attempts to reform by experience what is the chief glory of reason. It is a vision fixated on experience and more suited to the blind ignorance of a mole than to a being who was created to stand upright and contemplate the heavens.
>
> In our times, so rich in words and poor in deeds, this maxim creates. . .the greatest of harm. For this concerns the canon of reason (in the practical), where the value of practice entirely depends on its closeness to the theory

which underlies it, and all *is lost, when the empirical and accidental conditions of the law are made into preconditions of the law itself,* and so a practice which is calculated on the basis of its probable outcome according to *previous* experience is allowed to dictate the theory on which it itself is based.[21]

"Previous" is emphasised by Kant — and in fact here lies the danger of the "scandal of philosophy", of the pseudophilosophical polemics against philosophical values and philosophical ideals. "Everything is lost" argues Kant if philosophical value does not guide the theory of praxis. For if theory bases itself only on *previous* experience then praxis too can only build on *previous* experiences. With the aid of such theories what exists cannot be overcome, and the "everything" that is lost is the future of humanity.

However, to deny the values of the criterion of truth is more than a philosophical consensus of our time. This consensus is connected with the methodology of philosophy: a methodology is implied not only by the content of philosophical ideals, but also by the lack of ideals. This methodology is a "fragmentation" of language and speech into individual judgements. Certainly everyone knows that no such separation exists in people's actual thought, in their communication and in their theories and explanations of society. Equally, we know that an explanation, a train of thought, or even a social scientific theory (I will not mention the natural sciences for lack of competence) is value-laden, even if *not a single value judgement is used* in the explanation or in the theory. This however disproves the truth-claim of the separation of judgements of fact and judgements of value as little as does the relevance of the "isolation" of such judgements from one another. Philosophy always has the right to abstract from the facts and the right to confront them with *some or other Ought*. Not a single philosophy can be disproved, however many arguments one may bring against it which are justified in themselves. Only positivists claim that Aristotle or Kant are "long disproved". Not even the philosophy of the "scandal of philosophy" can be disproved. One can turn away from any philosophy. And although I do not believe that "everything is lost" if one does not turn one's back on this philosophy, I do believe that *much* is lost and that much becomes more difficult. For the Ought that is revealed in the reduction of the true to judgements of fact and in the methodological isolation of our judgements is the utopia of a completely isolated, atomised humanity, guided by no values whatsoever and controlled by "experts" or by the ideology of science. Let us therefore turn away from it.

We must rediscover our own true values; we must have the commitment for our theory to be again guided by "practical reason". Philosophy must put an end to the scandal of philosophy.

I have claimed that for every epoch it is revealing what philosophy it has, what the value is on which a consensus exists, how the ideals are understood, discussed and with what content they are filled. We would do our epoch an injustice if we did not *once again* stress that we live in a time in which philosophy is awaking to new life, even if it itself remains unaware that it is. The highest good is awaking to new life, it is again taking up its place in the pantheon of philosophy. What however is this highest good?

Wittgenstein left its role still open. Everything that was thinkable in what has been described as positivism he lived most grandly and most tragically and thought through to the end because he, as a true philosopher, kept the highest good undisturbed in the heaven of philosophy. Because he lived and thought *that* through to the end, for him the highest good remained inexpressible. It was Sartre's great deed once again to give this highest good a name: *freedom*. And today more and more freedom gains a new meaning. Here only one — to me very significant — interpretation: the rational utopia of the "ideal communication society" of Apel and Habermas. For what else could this ideal communication society be but the formulation of truth in the equality of free people and in the freedom of equally rational people?

It is therefore rational to constitute the true, the good and the beautiful, but not in order to gain an answer to questions

of "What does 'good' mean?" "What does 'beautiful' mean?",
for in this way one receives *no* answer. Rather it is rational
because one once again is posing the questions: "Is what you
hold to be good really good?" and "Is what you hold to be true
really true?" But such questions are always reasonable, for the
true, the good and the beautiful *are created by us as humans*. In
particular the ideals pose questions: Must our life be made as
you have made it? And they enjoin us: Make it better, more
true, more beautiful! Change life according to the meaning of
ideals which you yourselves have understood! And indeed,
nothing can be more realistic than these ideals, for there is no
greater reality than the impossible. Only a theory based on
these values of philosophy can produce a praxis which, to
recall Kant once again, goes beyond the "previous".

Now, however, back to the "guarantee" of philosophy. It
has been said that one cannot deduce one value orientation
category from another but that one can connect value orientation categories with each other; the "ideal" of philosophy is
the person who links the striving for the good with the striving
for the true. But it was also said that there is nobody who
strives for "the beautiful", "the good", "the true", *as such*. Or
is this so?

"I want to know the truth!" "I must know the truth!" "I
want to know what the truth is!" — Mere exclamations, with
which we are all familiar since we encounter them daily. When
Oedipus said he wanted to know the truth, he wanted to know
why the city had to suffer; he wanted to know what crime had
been committed and who was responsible for it; he wanted to
know what he himself was doing, whether he was acting and
leading his life according to the laws; he wanted to know what
he had to do *and whether and how he should alter his life* in order
to save the city. The exclamation "I want to know the truth!"
therefore goes far beyond the question whether or not something is or is not the case.

Somebody who wants to solve a mathematical problem or
assess experimentally an hypothesis never says "I want to
know the truth!" They want to know whether the chosen
solution is correct, whether it fulfils its purpose, whether the

experiment confirms the hypothesis. In such cases, in exceptional circumstances, the expression "I want to know the truth!" is also possible, but only when the solution to the problem has an immediate connection to morality and human conduct; if the "truth" that one demands challenges the dominant beliefs or if it cuts across one's own previous ideas and convictions, if a commitment to this truth means a break with public beliefs or one's own past — *if therefore "the truth" is at the same time "the good"* for which one is engaged and which one will proclaim. One therefore often heard this exclamation from those who still had to struggle against religion and not least against their *own* religious convictions.

The exclamation "I want to know the truth" does not mean that one strives for knowledge *for knowledge's sake*, but that one wants to be enabled with the help of knowledge to act *autonomously* and restructure judgements, facts and life itself if they ought to be restructured. In this context it is immaterial *what* one wants to know and how important it is. I want to know the truth! I want to know whether my friends betrayed me or not, and indeed, not to register the knowledge, but because I wish to judge them accordingly, because I want to act accordingly, because in my eyes eventually the value of "friendship" is changing because I will revalue it and give it a different content, because I want to change my mind. I want to know why there are rich and poor, whether there is a hereafter, who has committed this deed and for what reason, I want to know why this suffering exists in the world and whether it has to exist, I want to know why my people are hated, why this war is instigated — indeed, *I want to know the truth*.

Yet soon as someone exclaims "I want to know the truth", in this really very everyday exclamation *the good and the true are linked*, irrespective of whether it is a question of petty things or things of great moment. The "truth" is the true knowledge in relation to values, in relation to the good.

The person who exclaims "I want to know the truth" is the guarantee of philosophy. We know that it was the polis which created the two forms of objectification which offer an answer to the seeker after truth. We know why it was precisely the polis, and we also know that the two forms are the Judaeo-Christian religion and philosophy. Christ said, "I am the truth." Hence the ideal of the Christian religion (for it is obviously also an ideal): the person who follows Christ. Philosophy says, "Let us seek the truth together." Its ideal is therefore the rational being who thinks autonomously. Every original philosophy posits the ideal person as the generalisation of those who rationally seek the truth. If this guarantee did not exist, then the ideals of philosophy would be a sham and a fraud. The appeal to the species always means that the qualities of the species are being sought in the individual and that the appropriation of the values of the species is to be *through the individual*.

The philosophy which denies the most basic feature of all original philosophy, the highest good, is therefore for that reason alone a "scandal of philosophy", because it *cannot be related to the person who seeks the truth*. The exclamation "I want to know the truth" is specifically not about whether something is or is not the case, but about what the existence or non-existence of the case *means* for my life, for the life of humanity and for the problems of humanity. Anyone who claims that the choice of values is irrational turns their back on those who want to know the truth. Such a person can form a concept of human beings, but not an ideal of human beings, and for such a person then everyone would be equally close to or equally far from the god of philosophy. The "language", the "logic", the "facts" of neo-positivism are the *empty gods of immanence*. Here there is no "Consider how you should think, how you should act and how you should live". This philosophy does not address people who despite everything, despite the "scandal of philosophy", today still exclaim: "I want to know the truth."

SOCIAL VALUES AND INDIVIDUAL ACTION

We have attributed to philosophy value rationality, but as yet we have not defined more closely what we understand by value rationality. We have defended the claim of the founders of philosophy that they spoke of *true values* and constituted their values as truth, but as yet we have not taken into account the *collision* that results from all values raising the same claim to universal validity. Therefore we intend first to focus on the problem of value rationality, so that we can later consider the truth or falsity of values.

Today Max Weber's concept of the difference between value rational action and purposive rational action is well known and applies. We wish to use these categories, in particular that of value rationality, but with a slightly different meaning. We asssume that what values shape a given action depends not only on the attitude of the actors to the end and the values, but also by the *quality* of the action and by the quality of the end itself. People could never have had an "attitude" to relate all their action to the highest values, in other words, to orientate decisions and choices to the highest value. At the same time however, purposive rationality is not simply a question of "attitude" either; there are types of activity which required purposive rationality even when human activity was primarily "orientated" to values. We accept Max Weber's claim that in the bourgeois epoch purposive rationality has "absorbed" value rationality as a striking formulation of a *tendency*. By this we mean that purposive rationality extended beyond the types of activity to which it had earlier been related and had had to be related, and shaped *all* spheres and types of human activity. Thus the illusion was created that value rationality was "irrational".

In describing these concepts we return, at least for our starting point, to Aristotle. His categories are so "transparent" because he lived in a time when value rationality could not be doubted, but when purposive rationality had also emerged as a particular kind of rationality in relevant areas of human action. Aristotle describes purposive rational action with the term techné, that of value rationality with the term energeia; he separates clearly from each other the two types of activity to which he applies the one or the other term. Techné is creation, meaningful work worthy of the free person; energeia is social action.[22]

When I apply myself to the realisation of an end in creation

I do not any more raise the question of whether the purpose is valuable. In this situation I understand work as a technological process. The determination of the value content — the purpose of the work — is *not* part of the work itself but rather a part of social activity. In work the purpose is already "given": as an ideal aim in the heads of humans. Therefore my work is rational when I can choose the necessary means for the realisation of the given aim, and when with the help of these means I can realise the aim. The sole criterion of purposive rationality lies in the *realisation* of the given aim. The confirmation (and indeed the only confirmation) that my activity was successful is the appearance of the aim that was in my head as an object *that is as it is*. This Aristotelian model is doubtless the model of *all* purposive rationality. Therefore the solution of every task of a technical nature depends on purposive rationality. The problem in bourgeois society is not in fact that there are types of activity which can only be successfully realised if the value content of the aim is not questioned, but instead has to be accepted as given and attention concentrated exclusively on the selection of the purposive necessary to realise it. The problem is far more that this type of activity is preferred even when it is *unnecessary*, indeed even when it is *unacceptable*: it is uniquely unacceptable for the establishment of the goal itself.

The criterion for rationality in Aristotle's value rational action, energeia, is something *other* than that in purposive rationality. Value rationality is a characteristic of *social action*, of *interaction*, of *communication*. Certainly within value rationality one is also guided by differing intentions, but by ones which form a value relationship and which are values ascribed both by the society in which we live *and* by us ourselves. For example, if we have to defend our country against an aggressor or if we hold that slaves should be freed, then it is demanded of us that we use all our strength in this situation to observe the norm or to establish a law which we believe to be just. The value rationality of an action or of a series of actions does *not* depend in any way at all on whether or not the aim is achieved. Our deeds are no less value rational if the homeland in fact experiences a defeat, if the slaves are not liberated, etc.

There are two criteria of value rationality. First, that the actors *continually hold fast* to their values, and second, that this value itself enjoys social *recognition*.

From the standpoint of purposive rationality the task of the individual consists in *realising* an aim, but from the standpoint of value rationality it is in *maintaining* the value to which one has pledged oneself. Aristotle expresses this by saying that "energeia" really amounts to continual virtuous activity. If people cease to act according to a value and to an aim held to be valuable, then the value looses its validity and the realisation of the aim loses its value rationality. In this context, whether a value is rational or not hinges not on the "nature" of the value but on *us humans* who have chosen to observe it. Its rationality depends on whether we can act continually under its guidance, according to its meaning and for its realisation *In this sense* it is irrelevant whether or not the aim is actually achieved.

Here however we must pause for a moment. Within the category of value rationality we have also been considering value *choice*. If we isolate the aspect of value choice from the *totality* of the action and of the personality of the person concerned and from their relationship to the world, then the idea of value choice has no meaning. In the moment of choice one cannot be guided by *the* value one has chosen. This would require a logical fragmentation of the actions of a unitary personlity, and that is something we reject. If a person chooses a value his or her consciousness is not a "blank page". One always arrives at the choice of new values as the *consequence* of continually upholding particular values. The choice of new values is a free and conscious act, because it is an act of choice and decision. However, it is no way an act that is *independent* of previous value rational actions, and this act of choice *is itself an action*. At the same time however every value choice will subsequently confirm or disprove its own rationality. In so far as one subsequently continually acts according to the chosen value and with the intention of upholding the values, the choice *reveals* itself as *rational*; if one does not, then it can certainly be said that the value choice was "irrational" (although I myself would claim that this terminology has no meaning, since really in this case *no act of value choice has occurred*). A value which is not adequate to the function of guiding rational action cannot count as having been chosen. Doubtless values can lose their rationality, although this is completely independent of whether they are inherited or chosen values. Further, one can even claim that at least in dynamic societies values that are merely inherited lose their rationality more frequently than ones that are chosen.

The second criterion of value rationality is social recognition. As far as we are concerned, this refers not to the action, but to the value itself: society has to accept the chosen value as a value. This certainly does not imply any consensus of an entire epoch or society in relation to the form of a *given value*, but is mostly a question of a *representative consensus* (of a social class, stratum or community) which always expresses a given need. If today somebody were to choose acquiring slaves as a value, we could immediately claim that their value choice was irrational, even if people could be found who agreed with them. Yet for Aristotle this same belief counted as a value, indeed even as "art"! If today in Europe someone started to honour the cow as "holy", we would certainly not regard their value choice as rational, even though in India today cows certainly are holy because there this is a recognised value based on a social consensus. Europeans who stigmatise worshipping holy cows in India as "stupid" only prove their own stupidity: namely the fact that they know no other rationality than that of purposive rationality. Incidentally, it is characteristic of people in bourgeois society to classify value rationality as "stupidity" even in regard to values which are easy to understand and which are recognised in their own society. Decency, honour and truth count as "empty humbug" which the "clever person" dismisses. Can philosophy then be blamed if it understands value choice as irrational?

But nonetheless, this is *also* philosophy's fault. For as long as even *one* value enjoys social recognition and for as long as this is actively and continually upheld by just one person, then philosophy must uphold value rationality *as a value* and cannot classify value choice — any value choice whatsoever — as "irrational". There are countless values on which we agree, even when we from time to time put forward others, and there are not a few people who continually and actively uphold these values.

As the objectification of value rationality, philosophy cannot give up value rationality, for that would contradict its own definition. This certainly does not mean that it must also challenge purposive rationality when it is justified and when it is *in its proper place*. We consider it necessary to stress this, since for many the justified rejection of the contemporary dominance of purposive rationality could lead to the demand that one should again abolish the specificity of purposive rationality, or to an idealisation of primitive societies in which purposive rationality is not yet differentiated *within* value rationality. One meets this demand and this idealisation especially in romantic ethnographic literature, for example in Lévi-Strauss' work on myths. Doubtless in certain primitive societies the labour process itself was not purposive rational nor were the technical aspects of the economy separated from the values of the society, and doubtless today one can still find societies that are partly like this. However, if one starts from a sense of responsibility for the problems of our own times, then such a type of society can serve us neither as a model nor as an ideal. This is primarily because such a "model" could only be realised at the cost of the complete dismantling of modern industry and technology, and because the administration of large social entities without such a differentiation of purposive rationality would be impossible. One could perfectly well object here that this is only relevant from the point of view of our own value choice — because we do give priority to the dynamic in a society. This is a preference we do not wish to disguise, nor do we want to deny that we see the development of production as the essential condition of the future society. However, it is quite another question *what sort of development* and *what direction of development* we hold to be sensible for production; equally, we believe the content and the direction of the development should be decided by value rationality. Once however the direction of the development is fixed for a period of time by value rationality and by value discussion, then its realisation is inconceivable if at the same time purposive rationality is eliminated. Today humanity is no longer the mere sum of isolated or relatively isolated small units, but rather, given world communication, a unity which cannot be split into individual components. And in addition, today it is a question of four (and tomorrow perhaps six) billion people. Given these two factors, the future of humanity without purposive rationality or without the differentation of the purposive rational form of action from value rationality can only *even be imagined* as a vision of chaos and famine. Those therefore who glimpse in the period before the differentiation of purposive rationality some form of "golden epoch" cannot in any way put this forward as a rational utopia for humanity. However, let us return to the problem of value.

An epoch is not only characterised by the concrete hicrarchy of value orientation categories, in which at least in principle the orientation categories of good and evil always have primacy as the necessarily imperative categories, but also by the value hierarchy as such. The spheres, types of activity, objectifications, feelings, etc., to which we apply the different value orientation categories, and which therefore are values because they enter into a "value relationship", are "hierarchialised" in different ways. Normally the society lays down a particular value hierarchy, but this can be modified according to strata, communities and even individuals. It is a question of the *structure* of the particular society what room to manoeuvre is availiable for these modifications. The "fixed" value hierarchy, that is to say, the firmly fixed system of material values all mutually ranked one above the other, disintegrated with the emergence of bourgeois society: its re-creation is neither possible nor desirable. This however does not mean the collapse of *all* value hierarchies. The hierarchy can determine the "place" of the value, such as the place of loyalty in the moral value hierarchy, or the relations in which the value enters, such as to whom should one be loyal (to master, friend or cause?) and equally it can specify the meaning of the value, such as the meaning of loyalty (to whom is one truely loyal?). The vertical and horizontal ordering of all the values we term the *value system*.

Just like society, individuals are not characterised by a *single* value but by a *system* of *values*. Within this system many values are, at least in everyday life, morally indifferent and function merely as "instructions". In relation to the values of usefulness and pleasantness there is nothing "bad" about this: it would be bad if one had to chose them autonomously in every single case. If before washing one's hands one had to consider whether one chose the value of hygiene, then it would be impossible to survive. However, the higher a value stands, the greater is the role of morality in our relationship to it, and so the greater is the importance of our conscious decision for it. Values with a moral content are thus values which are distinguished by the fact that our active relationship to them contains a *moral aspect*. Such values cannot function as mere "instructions for use". That they cannot function as such means in no way that they do not de facto function as such, but rather that they ought not to do so. The rationality of these values is — from a particular point of view — created precisely by our conscious choice and by the continual activity which corresponds to it.

If we through an action *consciously* realise values or want to realise them, if we therefore proceed with a value rational orientation, then we do not necessarily choose the value that stands highest in the hierarchy, but rather a value *that is adequate to the given form of activity*. For example, Aristotle held generosity to be a value standing higher in the hierarchy of moral values than courage, but he would have found it absurd if in war somebody practised the virtue of generosity and not that of courage in relation to the enemy. Adequacy to the situation is an aspect of value rational action that cannot be eliminated, any more than can be adequacy to the subject, which can be eliminated from the standpoint of neither the acting subject nor the subjects with whom one acts collectively or whom the action affects.

Adequacy to the subject and adequacy to the situation are determined by several factors. Since an extensive analysis of them belongs to the sphere of ethics, we will content ourselves with a few examples. Since a part of value rationality is the continual upholding of a given value, when one judges the value rationality of a subject's action one cannot abstract from the value rationality of the same subject's *earlier actions*; when the subject however chooses a new value in an action, they must do so consciously and must explicate the value. Often two subjects carry out the same action, but from a moral standpoint this is not the same action. If someone acts on the basis of new values, wihtout considering them and without revising their earlier actions, then from the point of view of the acting subject the value rational action is *not* subject-adequate and is *not* the moral equivalent of a subject-adequate action. Alternatively, if somebody's passions conflict with their aims and the latter are held to be valuable, then their value rational action must be seen as *meritorious* and be given greater recognition; the assessment is subject-adequate from the point of view of the acting subject. Or, our loyalty too is in one way dependent on to whom or to what we are loyal. We can be loyal in that we unconditionally commit ourselves to a person or to a cause, or we can be loyal with distance and criticism. Whether we link loyalty to the value of unconditional acceptance or to that of criticism has to be determined by both the object and the circumstances of the loyalty — it has to be adequate to both the subject and the situation.

The fact that neither situation adequacy nor subject adequacy can be removed produces what we want to call *the dilemma of morality. It has to be remembered that good and evil are the pair of orientation categories which guide actions with moral content. Normally, if not in all areas of application, this pair of value orientation categories orders or forbids. That is to say, each use of these values takes the form of rules of action and behaviour* which must be obeyed. Morality is thus a system of rules which — in the case of conflict — *ought* to take precedence over all other systems of rules. Kant's categorical imperative formulates this imperative character of morality in that he assumes, as we do not, that the moral law contradicts all other systems of rules, so that to choose is at the same time to exclude.

Every value rational action has to be adequate to the situation and the subject and not just the object. From the point of view of morality, object adequacy means to *correspond* to the system of rules. The moment however that one acts, this system of rules is applied in a concrete situation and to concrete people. It follows from this that *we can certainly claim the universal validity of our moral values, but we can hardly claim the universal validity of our moral actions*. And the higher are the values on which we base our allegiance to the system of moral rules, the less we can make this claim. Maxims such as "Every person should have the right to personal freedom" or "Other people's needs should always be considered" can claim universality. If however on the basis of these values I decide to get divorced, then I cannot make any claim for the universal validity of my action. I cannot say that everyone who claims that every person should have a right to personal freedom or that the needs of others should be considered should get divorced. This would be absurd. Certain British moralists want to solve the dilemma of morality by arguing that everyone should act as they would wish anyone in their situation to act. This however is just as absurd. If we argue that no two leaves on a tree are identical, how can we then in any way claim that several concrete people in *one* concrete situation act in exactly the same way as several other concrete people in another concrete situation, let alone claim that they *should* act in exactly the same way? Every person is an unrepeatable individual, and every situation is an unreplicable individual process.

The concrete situation and the subject who acts, together with the person with whom the subject acts or whom the action concerns, frequently demand that one moral value is preferred to another without the latter thereby losing its claim to universal validity. The higher are the values which the action involves, the more common and the more unavoidable it is that one confronts this dilemma. If it is a question of washing one's hands before one eats, then I can confidently declare that *everyone* ought to wash their hands before they eat. If however I exclaim, "Thou shalt not kill", but kill people in war or vote against the hanging of a mass murderer, or if I proclaim justice to be a value but then as the occasion arises show mercy instead of justice, or in the name of justice show no mercy to a person pleading for mercy, then *in none of these cases* can I wish my *action* to have any claim to universal validity. Neither the choice of values nor value rational action can exclude the aspect of *personal responsibility*. The higher the value, the less this is possible. We are personally morally responsible for our choice of values and our value rational actions. Anyone who wants to eliminate the aspect of personal responsibility or individual choice from value rationality wishes to eliminate value rational action itself.

At this point I would like to return briefly to the idealisation of primitive societies. As we have seen, in such societies there is no pure and differentiated purposive rationality. However, this also means that there is no pure value rationality. The emergence of pure value rationality depends on the differentiation of means rationality. One recalls the "Not this is good, but that" or the "Not this is beautiful, but that" — the objectifications of value rationality have arisen due to the differentiation of value rationality.

The elimination of situation and subject adequacy from value rationality does not lead to confirming the universal validity of maxims, but to scandalising basic common sense. Kant had attempted it: the result is well known. If a murderer is looking for his victim, there is no reasonable and respectable person who, on the grounds that one should not lie, could claim that one should tell him where he would find him.

ALTERNATIVE FORMS OF LIFE, THE VALUE SYSTEM AND VALUE JUDGEMENTS

Earlier it was said that people do not act on the basis of a single value and that they are not guided by a single value. Instead their whole value system is at work and they have to observe values which are *also* adequate to the situation in which they act. Somebody who consciously chooses or reaffirms their value also has a conscious value hierarchy, but in it one or more values will have a dominant function, that is to say, will occupy the place of the "highest standing" values. We will term these the "leading values". The system of values is either coherent or incoherent, depending on whether or not there are contradictions between the leading values and the other values in the value hierarchy. A coherent value system is one without contradictions: every value is *subordinated* to, *related* to, or *indifferent* to the leading values. Everyone is *obliged* to *strive* to make their value system coherent.

Not every action is directly determined by the leading values. Nonetheless one has to try to ensure that the values which are decisive for the action do not contradict the leading values. This has nothing to do with what we earlier described as the "dilemma of morality". At the level of *value choice* there is no contradiction *at all* between "Thou shalt not kill" and love of the fatherland, nor between justice and mercy. They can all concurrently, in the same way and at the same time raise the claim to universal validity. In each case the contradiction results from the concrete situation. However, when the Kantian formula that no one should treat someone else as a mere means serves for someone as a leading value and that same person accepts violence, or when someone in the same breath advocates equality and inequality between the sexes, or democracy and the restriction of free opinion, then we can rightly speak of an incoherence of the value system. A well-known and typical example of an incoherent value system is the "doubling" of values in relation to action and to judgement, or in the application of values to theory and to practice. One of the most important issues within value discussion is proving the incoherence of a value system.

It was claimed that the incoherence of a value system has in itself nothing to do with the dilemma of morality. This however is only true in discussion of the problem *at the theoretical level*. As soon however as someone judges a concrete act and is confronted with the person who has been judged, then they will rationalise the actions that result from the incoherent value system with the help of the dilemma of morality, even when they have not heard of this dilemma. They will say,

"This is something quite different, the situation was in fact such and such, this is an exceptional case." Similar rationalisations are used by those who subordinate their values to their own particularity. Kant wanted to prevent this "rationalisation" by attempting to eliminate the "dilemma of morality" — at least at the theoretical level. He could however only actually do this by removing action from morality. Morality however precisely realises itself in action, and the process of realisation cannot be wished away from morality. We do not wish to deny that Kant's question is justified. The dilemma is a dilemma, *because it has no theoretical solution.* For anyone who makes a moral judgement (and once again, they are saddled with personal responsibility for it), it is their duty to differentiate between the realisation of a value, the incoherence of a value system and the rationalisation of their own particularity. *There is no general formula which could release them from this responsibility.*

We have described the dilemma of morality and have argued that although we claim universal validity for our values, we cannot claim any universal moral validity for our actions. The unavoidable basis of value choice and of value rational action, the claim to universal validity of the chosen values, stands at the centre of modern philosophical controversies over values. One could crudely sketch the proponents' positions by saying: one side puts forward the view that in itself the claim to universal validity reveals the irrationality of value choice. That is, values are not objective, for one person will choose this value and another that value. According to this argument, contradictory values oppose each other and each makes the same claim to universal validity. The values cannot be "true", if only for the reason that mutually opposing values all claim to be true. According to the representatives of this position, it therefore follows that a reasonable and successful value discussion is impossible: the subjectively chosen values face each other, each is immovable, value choice cannot be changed by arguments. The adherents of the opposing position want to retain the objectivity of values. Since however they accept, at least in many aspects, the arguments of the previous position, they attempt to ground the values transcendentally (Scheler).

The theoretical basis of the antagonism which emerges from the discussion of the universal validity of values is to be found, so we would argue, in the fact that the structure of value rationality is conceptualised as analogous to that of purposive rationality: its social basis is the structure of bourgeois society itself. Why this is so, we shall see later.

In order to avoid this dilemma, we must never lose sight of the basic criterion of value rationality. Above all, one must differentiate between *valid values and the concrete nature of the content of the valid values.* For the sake of simplicity we shall consider first the preferred pair of the imperative orientation categories themselves: *customary ethical values.*

The first thing to emerge here is that *a social consensus exists in relation to the leading moral values.* And this applies not to a given social "moment" but also to overarching historical epochs. Courage, honesty (honour), justice and friendship counted as leading moral values when it was held to be true knowledge that the speed at which objects fall depends on their weight. Goodness and love were leading moral values when knowledge of the horror vacui of nature counted as true knowledge. True knowledge of nature has undergone much greater changes than the truth of values has. To explain this circumstance however one needs neither God nor Platonic Ideas. People create their moral ideas themselves: the different moral values are not creations of one and the same social period, but rather have emerged continually. They do however have one unique feature: once they have crystallised, then they live on as *ideas*, because they retain their social recognition and people uphold them in their regular actions. It can happen that some values are moved lower and others higher within the hierarchy, but in any case the *invariable* values select themselves from these ideas. These values however have universal validity. To claim that they are universally valid is therefore neither arbitrariness nor subjectivism; it is simply to express their empirical universal validity.

It is not difficult to determine which moral values are universally valid. They are the values which morally relativise their opposites: their "opposite" can *never* have any claim to universal validity and can only gain acceptance as an exception. Consider for example justice. This value is universally valid and its validity does not require any further confirmation: nobody can choose *injustice* as a value. "Justice" has relativised injustice. I can say "In this particular case I must be unjust, because. . .", but I cannot say that I strive for injustice. The universally valid moral values *express humanity's species character*. This is the reason why the exceptional case of a deliberate choice of a non-value is always condemned as devilish. "I am determined to prove a villain" is a devilish principle. In the same fashion love has relativised hate, truth betrayal, sympathy indifference to suffering, courage cowardice. *From now on we shall term universally valid moral values "value ideals"*.

Our starting point was the moral sphere, for here we could most clearly explicate our own concerns: no single value ideal can be considered as an "archetype" and as given to people from birth; without exception all value ideals have emerged historically. Every single value could originally only be interpreted in *one* way. For example, courage meant courage in *war*. Later it was more and more generalised into an ideal endowed with different meanings and so became the centre of a value reference system of an epoch and of a cultural milieu. The centres of such value reference systems were not primarily formed by pure moral value ideals, but by those value ideals which also contained a moral aspect, a moral meaning and a moral interpretation. The value ideals which structure our time and our cultural milieu are freedom, personality, equality, happiness, humanity and human life. The majority of these value ideals are today accepted in all significant cultural milieus. It is in general the case that the more historical epochs they have existed in and the more cultural milieus they have been effective in, the less likely is their universal validity to be questioned. Thus, for example, nobody can openly say that their aim is the unhappiness of other people or that their leading value is the suppression or the destruction of personality. As for equality, it is incidentally the case that it in our cultural milieu it has not become a universally valid value to the same extent as freedom and personality.

The assumption that usually in value discussion universally

valid values stand opposed to each other is highly questionable. Moreover, it is quite *impossible* for *all* the values which
are held by two people and which claim universal validity to
collide with one another.

Normally collisions between values are in no way caused by
universally valid values, but by their *interpretations*. What for
example does freedom mean? The independence of nations,
freedom of thought, to do and to be allowed to do what one
wishes, or the free choice of the community? And so on. Or
take another example: what does life mean? The development
of biological life? The quality of life?

All our values are interpreted values. If we make claims for
their universal validity, then we do this at least for a concrete
meaning and for a particular interpretation. The
interpretation of a value always implies *a recommendation for
action that is right according to the value*. The purposes are
always fixed according to the *interpreted* value; it is this that
guides value rational action. In the same way we *make judgements and theories* on the basis of interpreted values. In
different interpretations the same values recommend quite
different and often even contradictory actions, and they are
frequently the basis for different *models* of society. Thus for
example A and B could say that for them equality counts as a
value. In A's understanding this means that every person
should have the same share of everything; by contrast in B's
understanding it means that equal people should have equal
shares in everything. The two interpretations of the same
value give two different recommendations for action, for
judgement and for the creation of theories, and they are the
basis of two different models of society.

Before we continue with our analysis, we wish to return
briefly to the contemporary controversies over value judgements. It was said that positivist thought analyses value choice
and value-guided action analogously to the schema of purposive rationality, and *hence* is not able to comprehend the
rationality of the former. One recalls here Aristotle's model of
purposive rationality: the plan of the house has been drawn up
and comprises our purpose — now we have to build the house.

The action is rational if *this* house is actually built. We have however seen that while in their actions people are certainly guided by a value, they understand this value very differently: depending on how they interpret it, they strive to realise differently evaluated goals under the guidance of the same value idea! From this it follows that one can never "realise" a value ideal: one cannot build "the house" of freedom or of equality. People struggle for different freedoms and immediately fill the idea contained in the word "freedom" with different meanings. The idea of the value is "maintained" by continual action which is related to it — it is through this that this particular action becomes rational. At the same time however it is possible that particular ends related to a value idea are never achieved, while particular interpretations can certainly be mutually exclusive. Once again this means that "the house" has not been built.

Against this background we can only repeat: the realisation of goals is not the precondition for value rational action. At the same time — and we will return to this again later — it is quite possible to *conceive* of quite different applications of the value idea being realised together. One cannot build a house if one starts on the cellar and the attic at the same time and if one "understands" the house in two different ways. In relation to values however this is not impossible, indeed it is normal. For example, if someone demands equal citizenship rights for women, someone else demands equal educational opportunities for the rich and for the poor, and a third demands the restructuring of the distribution of income in society in order to create more equality, then — to remain with the same analogy — the construction of the cellar, the second storey and the attic is being undertaken *at the same time* and from completely different points of view. None the less, all of this still refers to *one and the same value idea* — equality.

The "confusion" between the structure of purposive rationality and the structure of value rationality and the dominance of purposive rationality as the real rationality shows an affinity with the structure of bourgeois society. That is not to say that there is no value rational action in bourgeois society: bourgeois society was the first society to require a type of human being *who subordinates their whole life to an idea*: the citizen. Bourgeois society made the ideas of freedom, fraternity and equality into value ideas, and bourgeois society needed these ideas if it was to survive through the bourgeois revolutions and the national wars. At the same time the private bourgeois individual handed over both the determination of values and value rational action to the citizen. Bourgeois private life became more and more guided by usefulness. That is not to say that other values were not effective, but rather that their control function lost its "certainty". Values were relativised and rules reduced to rules of propriety. In pre-bourgeois society the validity of the values was, so to speak, "natural". In antiquity the guarantee for this was the fixed value hierarchy of the city community; in the Christian Middle Ages it was the ideal community (through the mediation of religion God was the indubitable source of all values and of the value hierarchy). It is easy to see that, despite all this, even in those periods no consensus existed over the interpretation of values. It is unnecessary to refer again to philosophy, but is enough to remember a well-known fact of everyday life — the Bible. The Sermon on the Mount, for example, was interpreted in very different and indeed in very contradictory ways. In bourgeois society however there is no community life and no community to lay down a firm value hierarchy. Although for religious consciousness God as creator of values has not ceased to be a "value guarantee", the majority of people have become atheists in their practice. Only to a continually declining extent does religion (if one leaves aside the sects) offer them a form of life. The belief that as an individual it is possible to choose freely one's values emerges at the same time as the idea of the value of freedom. The differences and the contradictions in the interpretations of values therefore produce the *appearance* that no guarantee exists for the validity of values. That is also the reason why writers and thinkers are once again concerned to restore, but only in this connection, the religious guarantee to its function — as does Rousseau in his famous allegory of the bridge of Poul-Serrho, or Dostoievski, who puts into the mouth of one of his heroes that if there were no God, then everything would be allowed. We have said appearance, meaning not an optical illusion, but rather the form of the appearance of the factual antinomy of bourgeois society. In a society which announces that people choose their values themselves and that value is a human creation, the majority of people have *no* possibility of participating in the creation of values but instead are excluded from it. An existential basis for value rational action, which places people in a position where they become conscious of the universal validity of values *without* any fixed value hierarchy and without any religious guarantee, can only be laid *when the determination of values is the common affair of all people*. So long as this is not the case, then there will always be a justification for interpreting value rationality as analogous to purposive rationality, for the appearance that value choice is irrational has not been removed.

We have said that the interpretation of value ideas and their filling with content can be very different; also that *every* action which relates to an interpretation is value rational action in so far as it corresponds to the criteria of value rationality (i.e. continuity together with recognition at least by a social stratum or community). In what follows however we have to distinguish between the values which ensure value rational action and *true* values. This is only possible if we formulate a criterion for the true value, for the nature of truth.

We live in a time with world-historical consciousness. The criterion of "true value" can therefore only be determined if we consciously reflect on this *historicity*. If we also put forward a criterion for the "true value", we do not wish to determine a criterion of the true value which is eternal and which is usable once and for all time, especially since any definition of such a criterion, even a subjective one, appears to us to be impossible. Our criterion therefore only applies to a period in which people choose their values themselves and also *know* that they are choosing them themselves. Those to whom the criterion of "true value" is addressed are also only those who test their chosen values and value interpretations in a *value discussion* and who are concerned to raise their value discussions to the level of a philosophical discussion. I therefore am making the criterion of true value a fact of a social process and I am making the need for this process into *an ideal of the true*, in that I explicitly *confront* it with the structure of existing society. In no way do I therefore deny, indeed on the contrary I insist, that for me the criterion of the "true value" is an ideal with which what is is to be confronted; it is something that *should* be striven for and *can* be striven for. Before I discuss this in more detail, I would like to clarify some preliminary conceptual points. Firstly, my philosophical theory of true value is *addressed to all* who want to overcome society based on relationships of superordination and subordination, repression and the inherited division of labour. However, I am *not* presupposing that there exists a social class or stratum from whose standpoint the creation of true values or the creation of theories of true values automatically occurs. Equally, I am *not* presupposing that those people to whom the theory is not directly addressed do not and cannot also strive for true values on the basis of the criteria which I am proposing in their own concrete value discussions.

Secondly, in my theory of "true value" I link *substantive* and *formal* value theory. I do this because I am convinced that if in the determination of the true value one does not proceed from a substantive, and thus universally valid, value, all our concrete values will become arbitrary, since the centre of our value domain will not itself be a value. In so far as a purely formal determination of "true value" is actually possible (and this I doubt), it cannot start from the human beings who are factually now acting with value rationality and explicating values. Therefore I reject this just as much as I reject a purely substantive determination of true value. The latter can only be ideological, because it is forced to recommend a "value code" which is held to be valid for everyone but which starts from the value domain, whether empirical or theoretical but in any case particular, of a particular stratum, culture or persuasion.

Thirdly, I will assign the "true value" to philosophical value discussion. In order to avoid misunderstandings: I choose the

category of "philosophical value discussion" not because I
believe that philosophers have discussed in this way. And yet I
find the expression correct. Philosophy starts from the
assumption that all people are equally rational beings and are
therefore capable of determining their values together in
rational discussion and of seeking the truth *together*. In our
theory therefore philosophical value discussion fulfils the
function of *the ideal*, the ideal on which the precondition
discussed above is based.

I characterise as *true value* that value which in particular can
be related *without contradiction* to the universally valid value
ideals, *and whose claim to validity does not at the same time
conceptually exclude the claim to validity of any other value that
can equally without contradictions be linked to the same value
ideal*. This can be formulated in the following way. It is our
duty to relate our values through such meanings and such
interpretations to the universally valid value ideals that their
general acceptance could be thought together with that of all
the other values that are related to the same value ideals but
that have other meanings. It is therefore our duty to elevate
our value discussions to the level *at which true values confront
true values*.

Let us start by considering the first aspect, which has the
formula: if one brings a value into relation with a value ideal
and there is then a contradiction between the value and the
value ideal, then the value is *not true*. If someone defends
slavery in the name of freedom, then without any more ado
one can explain that this value is untrue. If someone understands freedom in a way that allows them to do what they like
with the members of their family and rob them of their freedom, then one can certainly say to that person: your value is
not true.

Considered more closely, this first aspect already involves
the second. If we in fact say to somebody that slaveholding or
tyrannising the family do not in any way correspond to the
value ideal of freedom, so we at the same time presuppose
another meaning or other meanings of freedom. We presuppose that there is a meaning such as "Every person has an

equal right to personal freedom" which no other interpretation of freedom can contradict if it is to be recognised as a true value. Yet this first aspect really only contains the second in outline. In fact whenever someone points out the contradiction between defending slavery and freedom, and therefore proves from the value of the latter that the former is untrue, in order to formulate their value judgement they do not have to take into account all possible interpretations of freedom which do not contradict the idea of freedom as a value. "Every person has an equal right to freedom" is indeed not *one* interpretation amongst many of the value idea of freedom, but rather a universal justification of the value idea. *As interpretation* this interpretation has been elevated to the level of consensus. We therefore prove the contradiction between value and value ideal by comparing either an interpretation of the value ideal or a value to which the value ideal is related with the social interpretation of the same value idea. In this way the contradiction can be pointed out between the value and the value ideal — the fact that the value is untrue, mistaken, false or lost.

However, the second aspect of the true value goes beyond this. According to it the criterion for the true value is the fact that we relate it to the value ideals (above all to the idea of the value of the highest good — freedom) in such a way that it cannot contradict a single value interpretation which is related to the same value idea.

Above all we have to demonstrate why we characterise freedom as the highest good, that is to say, as the leading value idea within the list of our other value ideas. This above all because — today — freedom is a "complete" value idea, the universal validity of which nobody can question. Secondly, because values which cannot be related without contradiction to their *own* value ideal must also contradict the idea of the value of freedom. For example, if somebody explains that equality is to be achieved by a central authority deciding on the equal distribution of goods, then this value excludes a multitude of other interpretations related to the value idea of equality. From the point of view of the idea of the value of equality it is therefore not a true value; it is equally impossible for it to be related without contradiction to the concept of freedom. Or, to return to the discussion of the idea of the value "life". Whoever excludes the value "meaningful life for women" from their relation to the idea of the value "life" simultaneously robs woman of her freedom according to one of the interpretations of the idea of the value "freedom". That all discussion involving moral ideas of value *also* involve the idea of the value of freedom is self-evident.

But what does it mean when we say that the true value is a value which is related without contradiction to a value idea and which at the same time does not exclude the truth of any other interpretations which refer to the same value? As we have seen, it only means that *it is possible to conceive that all true values can be observed together*. Certainly *at the level of the present* the observance of the true values can be laden with contradictions. Indeed we know that because the ideas of value involve differing interpretations, they imply different recommendations in relation to action, the strategy of action, the form of life and the construction of theories. Further: *values that are equally true* can create strategies of action and of theory construction which in the present are mutually contradictory and mutually exclusive.

To speak of the "truth" of a value means however to recognise its right to universal validity. Every true value justifiably raises the claim to universal validity. The level of universal validity is however the level of what *ought to be*, not the level of universal validation in the present. If we explain that contemporary values which imply contradictory practical and theoretical decisions are conceivable together at the level of what ought to be, then we must also recognise that they are equally true and that they have the same claim to universal validity. And this is so even though the actions guided by their observance are different and often even mutually exclusive.

A value is therefore true if it can be validated together with *all* similarly true values. That is to say, it is conceivable that these values can be universally observed together at the level of what ought to be — the level of "what should be done", the level of being which is placed in the future. Thus for example today *development* is a valid value. One can understand "development" as the development of the forces of production, as the development of culture and of human relationships to a higher level, as the development of communities. Yet all these interpretations *can* be true values together, at the same time and to the same extent, because even if they involve different emphases, forms of action, attitudes and theories, their common realisation in the future is conceivable.

I said *can* be, and not that they necessarily are. In order to ensure their equal truth they have to be *interpreted* in such a way that the interpretation of one does not *exclude* the others. For example, if I understand the development of the productive forces in a way that excludes, even at the level of what ought to be, the development of culture or of the community, so that even purely conceptually the simultaneous achievement of all three values is no longer possible, then my value is *no* true value. It cannot be true, simply because it cannot be related without contradiction to the highest good, to freedom, for with my interpretation of freedom I am excluding other interpretations of freedom.

The creation of true values *ought* to be striven for. Hence, without abandoning the observance of a value, it is our duty to make our value interpretations conceptualisable together with all other value interpretations whose representatives recognise our value as a true value. For example, anyone who stresses the development of community *must* formulate this in such a way that at the level of what ought to be it does not rule out the development of the forces of production. Such a person can only say that the forces of production should not be developed in the manner, direction and tempo that they have been up to now, but instead in a tempo and direction determined by the community. The person who demands the development of the forces of production, *should* do this in such a way that the interpretation does not exclude the development of the community; they can only say that the structure of communities should not allow the productive forces of humanity to decay, but should rather ensure their development.

A value discussion is therefore completely possible in which true values face true values. Equally, a value discussion is possible in which on both sides the values of the opponents *raise themselves to the level of true values.*

We are well aware that in the determination of "true values" we have left unresolved one important problem, namely *the collision of value ideals themselves.* These collisions never involve value ideals in their entirety. Since value ideals have developed historically, again and again we see new value ideals emerging in times of great historical crisis. That is to say, particular value interpretations elevate themselves to the "rank" of a value ideal, but this elevation is always originally a process or a tendency. Even "freedom" and "equality" have not sprung from history like Athene from the head of Zeus.

At this point however we must return to philosophy.

We know that philosophy creates its own ideals that are both concrete and universal from value judgements such as "Not this but that is true" or "Not this but that is good". As an objectification with a utopian structure it often objectifies the claim to the universal validity of new values. Certainly philosophy does not choose its values out of nothing, but rather from already existing and already formed values. *Yet it makes those values which are related to value ideas into actual value ideas.* Philosophy is the vehicle through which new value ideas are formed and a new consensus over value ideas is created.

Two qualifications should be made to this argument. First, not every philosophy can fulfil this task, but rather only philosophies which have come into existence at the time of world historical changes. Second, philosophy does not always succeed in this enterprise. It is well known that up to Kant much of bourgeois philosophy wanted to make usefulness into a universal value and to identify it with the good. This attempt failed even in its selection of the value. Usefulness was an effective value throughout the whole bourgeois epoch, but never elevated itself to the level of a value idea. We do not relate other values to usefulness, but rather relate *it* to other value ideas; something is useful to the nation, to culture, to people, to development, etc. However, the highest good of bourgeois philosophy, freedom, did in fact elevate itself to the level of a value idea.

If within a value idea there are two value interpretations — that is to say, two values related to the value idea — which cannot be validated at the same time *through interpretation*, then philosophy has to *elevate them to the level of the idea of value*. Alternatively, in so far as it strives to transcend the antinomy in the structure of society, it has to elevate *one* of them into a value idea *in order* to relativise the other.

This raises the question whether two values exist within our contemporary interpretations of "freedom": values which are diametrically opposed to each other and which therefore contemporary philosophy should elevate into value ideas. Or alternatively, in so far as philosophy strives to transcend the antinomy in society, should it elevate one of them into a value idea and relativise the other?

I believe that two such diametrically opposed values do exist: namely the value of individualism and the value of community. It is enough to recall Nietzsche to show that it is not impossible to elevate both of them into value ideas. Since I will return to this issue, in order to avoid misunderstandings I shall admit that I myself an committed to the value of community and thus relativise the value of individualism. At the same time, now as before, freedom is the highest value. I have therefore linked the idea of "highest value" primarily to freedom. I therefore want "community" to be a value idea which, however it is interpreted and understood, cannot contradict freedom. *"Community" must not contradict freedom of the personality*. This follows automatically from what has been said already. Freedom of personality is the primary interpretation of freedom and as such itself functions as a value idea. The value which I wish to make into a value idea is not "community" by itself, but rather "community of free people".

For me this value idea that I am putting forward is *also* related to philosophical value discussion *as a value*. As I have already said, I consider my criterion for the true value to be addressed to those who strive for a philosophical value discussion (i.e. the discourse between true values) — it is addressed to those who today exclaim: "I want to know the truth!" However, philosophical value discussion as an ideal involves a world in which *everyone wants to know the truth*, in other words, in which everyone participates in philosophical value discussion and in choosing and determining values.

With this conception I openly endorse the common ideal of Apel and Habermas of an "ideal communication community". However, one can immediately see that what I propose as the contemporary criterion of true value differs fundamentally from Apel's proposal and even more from that of Habermas. That is, for them the truth of values — in practical and theoretical discourse — consists in "true consensus". A value would thus be true if there was a complete consensus about it. The concept of true value is accordingly also *counter-factual* in so far as it can only exist as never-ending progress within the never-ending theoretical and practical value discussion.

I cannot accept this conception for two reasons. First, I posit guiding values on which a consensus exists as *preceding* philosophical value discussion. That is, without such a consensus the true values cannot be assumed to be related to any authority: for a value discussion even to be possible, the communication community has to be guided by values. Second, in my opinion consensus is not in principle a criterion for the truth of values: the criterion is "only" that it must be possible to relate them without any contradictions to a universally valid value. In the determination of "true value" the *formal* criterion also expresses a preference: I decide for the *plurality of forms of life*. On the basis of my own criterion I can also confirm this value as a true value, for the value "plurality of forms of life" can be related without any contradictions to the universally valid guiding values of freedom, community and personality. My criticism of Habermas' theory is not that it is counter-factual. It is precisely an ideal, a philosophical ideal, and its counter-factuality is at the same time its justification. Rather my problem is that I cannot accept it as an ideal. I do not choose complete consensus as an ideal; I do not choose as an ideal a value discussion which makes it impossible for true values to oppose each other. I do not want there to be only one "true" interpretation of *Hamlet*, or there to be only one "good" form of life. It is for this reason that I have defined the "true" value in the way that I have, and it is for this reason that I recommend my criterion for philosophical value discussions and recommend it to all those who "seek the truth".

I certainly do not claim to be putting forward something like a general and "eternal" criterion for defining the "true value", but I do certainly claim that my criterion is not selected arbitrarily. In this connection I would like to recall my preceding remarks summarising the common traits of the ideals of "true" and "good" in all philosophies. In what follows I would like to show that they are all contained in the criterion by which I have defined the true value in contemporary value discussions.

The true is always *knowledge* as opposed to *opinion*. True knowledge is chosen and we consciously relate it to universally valid values. It presupposes that we "search for the truth": therefore that we question what is merely given, what is opinion or prejudice.

The true guides us in cognition and in action. The function of the true value is also theoretical as well as practical. With the help of true values or systems of true values we structure all our knowledge of society, of our past and of our present. At the same time in all spheres of activity we relate all our social action to true values. True values therefore fulfil two types of function — a theoretical and a practical one — which cannot be completely separated from each other because they are rooted in the unity of the personality.

"True knowledge" is our *reliable* guide in cognition and action. Without a true value to guide them our cognition and our deeds would not be assured of any certainty. This has not always been the case. Wherever "natural" community life is tightly woven and shapes people's whole existence, then action and judgement can be certain merely by "taking over" and applying the norms of the milieu. However, in a society in which the system of prescriptions has decayed into "roles", in a society in which there is no natural community which guides the whole of human life, none of this type of certainty of action and of cognition exists. Kierkegaard very appositely characterises the personality in the aesthetic phase who lacks any autonomous values as guides: "Marry, and you will regret it; do not marry, and you will also regret it; marry or don't marry — you will regret both; either you marry or you don't marry — you will regret both."

The striving for true knowledge is a theoretical orientation which demands the transcendence of particularity. The striving for true value also involves this theoretical orientation: "I want to *know* what truth is." Only the true value is able to "structure" our personality and give our action certainty. Anyone who searches for the value motivated by this consideration has not however overcome their particularity: the search for the true value always has to be the primary motive, without any reference to personal needs. If this is not so, then a person cannot reach the true value but instead they will rationalise as true every value which confers certainty on their deeds.

The good is always a value which contains morality, either as a precondition or as a justification. True values are values that are either universally valid or that can be related to universally valid values: they therefore always involve morality. Action that is related to true values demands, as does every value rational action, the continual upholding of a value with moral content. To the extent that it contradicts the realisation of the value, particularity has to be set aside.

Both the true and the good are expressed with conviction. For both the true and the good we accept responsibility. We take on responsibility for our true values.

To know the good to be a value is a fact of reason. To justify our true values we must therefore argue rationally. This presupposes, firstly, that we listen to and consider the counter-arguments, and that in the light of the counter-arguments we again and again examine whether the values that we have chosen are actually true. Secondly, it means that we recommend our values to every rational being; we therefore recommend our values as universally valid values.

Why, however, should we recommend them as universally valid? Because we only designate as a true value a value which can be related to a universally valid value idea without any contradictions. However, several values can be related to one and the same universally valid idea of value. These values — the definitions and interpretations of the meaning of universally valid values — can even factually contradict each other at the level of experience. Yet at the level of what ought to be — and this is precisely what matters as far as their universal validity is concerned — one can imagine how they could be validated together. One can therefore express them *all* and claim for them universal validity.

All true values are constituted by human beings. *Everyone* who seeks the truth and who therefore wants to participate in philosophical value discussions *has* to recommend true values to which they are committed.

If on the basis of a chosen value, I wish to enter into a *theoretical* discussion, then I can do so with the following formula: "I myself take responsibility for the values which guide me in my cognition and in my value judgements. I have examined my motives on the basis of the criterion of truthfulness, and can in good conscience claim that the value which guides and constitutes my theoretical work and my value judgements has not developed out of my private interests, my wishes or my needs. It does not rationalise these. Rather I have chosen it from valid values or have related it without any contradictions to valid ideas of value. I also take responsibility for organising according to my values the facts and the events in my theory, in my evaluations and in my value judgements, so that they have become facts of my theory while corresponding to the criterion of factual truth. I have listened to the arguments which have been brought against my values, I have considered them and have rejected them. Therefore I claim with conviction that my truth has universal validity. You too should think and judge in the same way!"

If on the basis of a chosen value I enter into a *practical* discussion, this is possible for me on the basis of the following formula: "I take responsibility on myself for the values on the basis of which I proceed and which I recommend for action. I have examined my personal motives on the basis of the criteria of truthfulness, and can in good conscience claim that the guiding value which I recommend for action and which guides my conduct has not developed out of my private interests, my wishes or my needs, and it does not rationalise them. On the contrary, I have chosen it from valid values or have related it without any contradictions to valid values. I vouch for this value having a positive value form, and guarantee that choosing it and observing it results from deciding for the value orientation category of the good in contrast to all other value orientation categories, and that it therefore has imperative character. It is this that should be done. I recognise it as my *duty* unconditionally to observe this value, and take this duty upon myself. I have listened to, considered, and rejected the arguments which have been made against my value. Therefore I claim with conviction that my truth has universal validity. You too should judge and act in this way!"

And so we have reached the stage of value discussion.

4

Communication

Only very rarely do value discussions occur about or between *value ideas*. The cases in which this does happen we shall call *"discussions about values"*.

The overwhelming majority of value discussions — the value discussions proper — are about the *definition* of the meaning of ideas of value, that is to say, about the *interpretation* and the *validation* of universally valid values. Even discussions about values must always refer back to concrete value discussion. In this reference back, the appeal to the facts which have been structured by the values plays just as important a role as the appeal to the task and to the relevant concrete situation. One person says, "I reject violence" and the other responds, "Do you condemn it in this situation and in this case?" or "What would you do in this situation and in this case?" or "What would you do in such a situation?" The answer could be: "I also condemn it in this situation and in no circumstances would I use it." But it also could be: "In that situation I do not condemn it and would use it." A further possibility is: "I also condemn it in that situation, but would however use it." In other words the person openly takes responsibility upon themselves for the dilemma of morality and admits that their action does not have any claim to universal validity, but that their value does. The moral value-world is coherent. In this last case, the responsibility the person is taking for their action is at its greatest.

This example makes the following clear: as far as the definition of the meaning of values in relation to their validation is concerned, in a discussion about values the reference to the concrete value discussion *theoretically* does not have to be linked to the dilemma of morality. In practice however the situation is rather different. Very often the dilemma of morality leads to the values becoming incoherent. In perspective, and therefore from the point of view of the present, this theoretical specification is unavoidable. It is even extremely important. *For we can imagine a society in which all the values that guide people are true values* which can be coherently related to ideas of value; *yet we cannot imagine any society in which the dilemma of morality ceased to be a dilemma*, in which therefore all actions guided by values could make a claim to universal validity. Class societies confront us with conflicts in which the dilemma of morality almost "forces" values to become incoherent. By contrast, in the society which we are proposing, upholding values that are true for us and adequate to both the situation and the subject will still result in the dilemma of morality. However, while this will hardly be without its tensions, it will not involve the same pressure for rationalisation.

And one further comment. Up to this point the problem of the validation of ideas of value has only been considered from the point of view of the "true value", in other words when a value — in a concrete and particular interpretation — is being observed. This however is usually an exception. The expression "the exception rather than the rule" has consciously been avoided, for where it is a question of the good, there *the exception can also be the rule*, and so it is in this context. As far as the social "average" is concerned, one can certainly say that there exists a contradiction between the validity of the values and their observance. We can observe abstract values through the observance of concrete moral norms. In addition, we have numerous concrete norms which involve no abstract norms (for example, rules of politeness), and also factually our action is guided not by norms which we recognise as true, but by motives which Kant described as "thirsts": above all "thirst for possession", "thirst for power", "thirst for fame". Therefore, in most value discussions true values are not in debate, since the interpretation of values is guided by intersubjective or completely individualist rationalisation of the passions. For this reason the system of values is *structured contradictorily, fragmentarily, and unreasonably*. These values occur at the level of "opinion" — to use a philosophical term — and they are therefore particularistic. Let us recall what was said of the socio-theoretical reception of philosophy. While the social theory — or any coherent train of thought, account, description, newspaper article, speech, etc. — is not guided by philosophical values, it is nonetheless based on values. And these values are particular, incoherent and unreflected; they are values which "opinion" rigidifies or which rationalisation produces.

To the question whether value discussion is possible and whether one can argue for one's own values or against other values, I reply: *value discussions do exist*, every day we de facto argue for and against values. Certainly however we do not argue *for every value* and we do not argue *against every value*, and we do not *always* argue.

Every *actual* value discussion is *limited* in time and space. *Theoretical* value discussion can be conceived as unending in time, while practical value discussion cannot. Practical value discussion bears either on recommendations which refer to action or directly on action itself, so inevitably it occurs under pressure of time. When we choose a value which guides action or when we choose an interpretation of such a value, then we must come to a decision within a given length of time if we are to act at all. For different types of action this period of time can be quite different, but this is another issue altogether.

In *theoretical* value discussion the conclusion is always relative, for the discussion can be continued at any time. In *practical* value discussion the conclusion is not relative, since we will be acting according to the value interpretation which has emerged "victorious" out of the argument. The controversy over the value can certainly flare up again, but not however still as *this* practical discussion, but instead as a theoretical value discussion, or as an argument in a *new practical value discussion*.

A value discussion can end in one of the following ways: (a) one partner is influenced by the arguments of the other, accepts the value that they are advocating and adopts its standpoint; (b) one partner accepts the value of the other as *probable* and decides to "test" it (this result can only occur in a practical value discussion, never in a theoretical value discussion or in a discussion about values); (c) one of the partners appeals to an indisputable authority to which the other submits; (d) the discussion ends inconclusively.

The relationship between the people who engage in a value discussion can be either symmetrical or asymmetrical. In the case of a symmetrical relationship the participants face each other as *equals* — as equally reasonable beings who in the discussion perform *equal* speech acts. Habermas terms this relationship an "ideal speech situation". However, the circumstance that equal individuals are performing equal speech acts is not, in itself, any guarantee that they will only use reasonable arguments in the discussion. It merely guarantees that neither of the opponents has any social power over the other, so that neither of them is able to break off the value discussion with an order based on the authority of power. Nonetheless, it is still possible for the value discussion to conclude with a resort to authority, for example, to the authority of God. If, for two equally rational beings, God counts as the highest representative of value and as the highest guarantee of a value discussion, then the symmetrical relationship does not exclude any resort to God's command. Therefore the "ideal speech situation" does not amount to the ideal needed for a value discussion; for this reason we define value discussion as the same as *philosophical* value discussion.

POWER RELATIONSHIPS

Asymmetrical relationships are ones of subordination and superordination. People who are subordinate or superordinate within the social division of labour, and within the systems of customs and institutions which codify it, cannot perform the same speech acts. Subjects cannot order the king to do something, they can only request him to do it. In the authoritarian family husband and wife, or parents and children, do *not* use the same speech acts with each other. In certain societies the relationships of subordination and superordination can even *rule out* value discussion. Yet even when this is not the case, the possibility always exists that one partner in the discussion ends it thanks to their authority. This obviously does not mean that it is meaningless or necessarily irrelevant for a subordinate to hold a value discussion with their superior. On the one hand, one cannot exclude the possibility that the other person will be convinced. On the other hand, continuing the argument can frequently validate other values, even very important values, such as courage, human dignity, etc. It is also not unusual that people who are bound to each other in an asymmetrical relationship can "suspend" this relationship for the duration of the value discussion. In such cases a person says "Let's talk man to man", which is only to say that in other situations they would not talk to each other in this way. Such a "suspension" is however always relative and at the same time problematic — only the court jester can tell the king the truth. From this perspective the institution of the "court jester" deserves special analysis. In any case, that it became an institution shows that even a person who is placed above others, and thus has no "symmetrical" relationships, needs someone with whom they can carry out a reasonable value discussion. Yet this person must stand outside the system of relationships of subordination and superordination; therefore he is a "jester". His arguments can never be taken seriously — one cannot answer them with the voice of authority — for his *person* cannot be taken seriously. Naturally the case of the king is an extreme example. In societies which are based on relationships of subordination and superordination, symmetrical relationships do also exist: people who are on the same level of social inequality stand in symmetrical relationships with each other. Yet these can *never be generalised* to the society as a whole.

Personal relationships of dependency can also be asymmetr-

ical. If these personal relationships of dependency are constituted as ones of subordination and superordination, then discussion will necessarily be carried on in different speech acts.
From this perspective there is no difference between the
relationship of the landlord to his own serf and his relationship
to another's serf, and vice versa.

Personal relationships of dependency are however *not only*
formed within relationships of subordination and superordination, but also by following an *aim*, or fulfilling a *task*. These
can be institutionalised, but they can also be spontaneous.
Even in a non-authoritarian family, small children are in a
relationship of personal dependency on their parents while
they are being "brought up" to socialisation and to an independent place in society. If one wants to achieve a goal, then
one can *oneself elect* or re-elect a relationship of dependency:
one elects for oneself a leader, a representative, a commander,
and thus one constitutes one's own personal dependency for
the duration of the task. One chooses to submit oneself, in
other words, to a *relative authority*.

There is such a great variety of personal relationships of
dependency that we shall not analyse them in detail. It merely
should be noted that personal relationships of dependency are
not necessarily relationships of subordination and superordination. This is not the case when every individual in the
relationship can participate as an equal in theoretical and
practical *value discussion*. At the same time, in relationships of
personal dependency not everyone has the same competence *to
participate equally in selecting the means for purposive rational
action and in working out the strategy for goal-realisation*. One
merely needs to consider a factory under democratic management. *Democracy* here has to involve the values that guide the
course of production being decided by the entire collective in a
rational value discussion. However, *management* is expressed
by the fact that realising the aim that the values have determined must involve relative authority. All the members of a
society *should* decide on its values and on which material
resources are to be used to realise them, and they should do so
in a rational value discussion. Yet an entire society can never

decide exactly how and with what means this is to be applied. That is to say, value rationality requires no specialised' expert knowledge, but yet in every case it does require value-neutral action. Let us recall Aristotle's simple example: merely in regard to the technology with which the house is to be built, not everyone is equally competent. Every member of a society is equally competent to decide whether the death penalty or even prison should be abolished, but working out the legal aspects must be left to the experts. Yet when one gives some-body responsibility for something, in that concrete situation one has endowed them with a relative authority. This means that as long as they are realising the goal that has been chosen collectively in rational value discussion, or as long as the value is not altered in a renewed value discussion, then one has to subordinate oneself to their expert knowledge. Without the relative authority in purposive rational action, a complex society could not function at all.

One can imagine a society without relationships of subordination and superordination, but a society that is anything more than a primitive one is unimaginable without relationships of personal dependency. A society is conceivable in which every value discussion is based on solely symmetrical relationships, but one in which controversies over purposive rationality are based on symmetrical relationships is not. When it is a question of purposive rationality, expert know-ledge always has the greater *weight*.

It is quite a different issue that in bourgeois society types of value rational activity charateristically function as though they were purposive rational, and hence are entrusted to "expert-ise", when in fact every educated and rational person, quite independent of their occupation, is equally able to cope with them. The aim must be to stimulate rational discussion of what necessarily belongs in the realm of purposive rationality and of expert knowledge — and from which therefore personal dependency cannot be eliminated — and what does not. To take a simple and illuminating example. If teachers of English use their authority to decide what a pupil's opinion of a literary work should be, then they are making a relationship of personal dependency into a relationship of subordination and superordination. If however it is a question of correcting false facts or grammatically false sentences in the pupil's essay, then they must proceed authoritatively: this case belongs in the realm of purposive rationality. The pupil cannot question whether 5 × 5 actually does equal 25. In every question that is not orientated to values, expert knowledge must count as the authority. All this can doubtless only be concretised so clearly and so unproblematically at a general level, but this must satisfy us here.

THE DILEMMA OF MORALITY

There are only two forms of value discussion: the *everyday* and the *philosophical*. However, the overwhelming majority of value discussions, which are moral, ideological and political, or concerned with the form of life, *constitute a transition between the two types*. They ascend from an everyday value discussion to a philosophical value discussion, or they descend from a philosophical to an everyday value discussion, or the opponents take up positions at different "levels".

In everyday value discussions it is not necessary for the values which are being discussed to have been consciously chosen or re-chosen; philosophical value discussions by contrast are concerned with consciously chosen or re-chosen values. To participate in everyday value discussions one does not necessarily have to have true values. Anyone who enters into such a discussion will not have purified their values from particular and personal motives, and the values may well be merely rationalisations of particular wishes and concerns. Yet they must contain a reference to certain values — ones accepted by the consensus as true — for otherwise a value discussion would simply be impossible. By contrast, in a philosophical value discussion the opponents should commit themselves to true values. In everyday value discussions the system and the hierarchy of the values can be latent; in philosophical value discussions the system and the hierarchy of the values should be explicit.

Every rational being should strive to hold their value discussion at the level of philosophical value discussion. The philosophical value discussion is therefore the *regulative idea* of all value discussions. The practical application of this regulative idea means at the same time the theoretical application of the same idea.

In societies which are based on subordination and superordination philosophical value discussion cannot be generalised. Here we can only locate this antinomy; we will return later to the problem of whether or not it can be dissolved.

As- far as the practical application of values is concerned, philosophical value discussions — like any value discussion whatsoever — take place under the pressure of time and the need for action. From a theoretical perspective we only put the individual under pressure of time: the ideal community of the partners in the discussion, humanity itself, is in principle not subjected to it.

The "leading up" to philosophical value discussion — that is to say, every discussion in which we justify our values as true values — can come to a relative conclusion. One discussion partner convinces the other that the value with which they entered the discussion was not a true value; they thus at once give a new meaning to their own value, so that it becomes a true value. Alternatively, the discussion ends inconclusively; this means the attempt to raise it to the level of a philosophical value discussion has failed. At the same time it is also possible in this value discussion (although only in its practical form) that one discussion partner accepts the value — the value interpretation — of the other as probable and tries it out. This however does not mean the discussion has *ended*, but only that the value discussion has been *postponed*. In the "leading up" to philosophical value discussion *there is no authority on which one can fall back*.

In philosophical value discussion the *truth* of the values is not being debated, for both partners recognise the truth of the other's value. Instead the discussion concerns far more the *hierarchy* of the values. It therefore concerns the question of which true value should be the leading value for our actions and for our conduct, and the question of on the basis of what kind of action we should accordingly constitute our social theory as the theory of our strategy of action. Since the decision in favour of one value always involves the subjection of another value — one which we nonetheless recognise as true — then, if the discussion is a practical one, every philosophical value discussion between values produces and reproduces the *dilemma of morality*. If the discussion is purely theoretical, then it expresses nothing other than the plurality of forms of life, the uniqueness of personalities, and the unending possibility of misunderstanding understanding.

Every rational being that has lived before us participates — symbolically — in philosophical value discussions. However, contrary to what Habermas claims, future rational beings do not participate in them, even symbolically. All the time we create our values from the values that exist, we relate them — if with a new content — to the existing values and value ideas, we interpret the existing values and value ideas. We desire the values that we choose to be valid for everyone, both in the present and in the future. Yet we also know that as other humans we ourselves construct our values. And we cannot rule out that — in the future — someone or other will strive for the universal validity of *other* values or of other values *in addition* to our own. We must assume that the people of the future will also form other values. However, we cannot rationally discuss what we do not know, for we do not exist *outside* history.

Our value system involves basic and derived values, all of which stand in a hierarchical order. There are no two people all of whose values, interpretations or value hierarchies would be *completely* identical. If there were two such people, then a value discussion between them would be impossible: there would be *nothing* which they could discuss.

We could posit as a limiting case two people, in whose value systems *not a single value* in one's system corresponded to a single one in the other's. Assuming that two such people did exist, then a value discussion between them would also be impossible: there would be nothing *with which* they could discuss.

Value discussions are possible, if: (a) the value ideas are the same, but yet their interpretation is different; (b) the values include some with the same interpretation; (c) the value ideas include some with similar interpretations; (d) the difference between the value systems largely results from the difference in the value hierarchies.

The fact that philosophical value discussions can be held does not mean to say that they actually will be held. An essential precondition for any effective discussion is that the partners — representing different values — *want* to hold a philosophical value discussion. *All* the potential partners must desire this. If directly or indirectly power is used to oppose arguments, then a value discussion is impossible.

The starting point of philosophical value discussion is always *hypothetical*. It is preceded by everyday value discussions in which people can clarify their values and can also be preceded by value discussions "ascending" from everyday discussions to the philosophical. In relation to the pure model the starting point is always an important factor, since we participate in philosophical value discussion with our *true* values. It is however part of our commitment to the "true values" to have heard and considered the arguments against our values. Therefore it is — from the standpoint of the pure model — necessary that philosophical value discussion is preceded by other — everyday or "ascending" — value discussions.

Concrete value discussions do not begin at the philosophical level. However, they can become philosophical ones in that, in the course of argument and counter-argument, the opponents mutually *raise* themselves to the level of philosophical value discussion. This can occur in the following ways: (a) a discussion partner, or a group of discussion partners, proves that in the value system of the other partner or partners there is a *contradiction*; (b) a discussion partner or group of discussion partners prove that in different judgements the other partner or partners are giving the same value *different meanings*; (c) a discussion partner proves that there is a contradiction or a discrepancy between the theoretical and the practical application of the other partners' value; (d) a discussion partner proves that the others in their theories are appealing to facts which do not exist and which cannot be replaced by others that are functionally equivalent in relation to the theory's coherence; (e) a discussion partner proves that on the opposing side a social event, an occurrence or an objectification, is being interpreted on the basis of the chosen values, in such a way that misunderstanding does not involve understanding; (f) a discussion partner proves to the others that there is a discrepancy between a particular *explicit* value and another *implicit* value.

It seems superfluous to say that — since the discussion is precisely a discussion — all this can also occur in the opposite direction.

To those who speak of the "hopelessness" of value discussion I would like to stress that the forms of argument enumerated above *in almost every case are effective and do convince, so long as the person to whom they are addressed is open to philosophical value discussion.* A true event can serve as an example.

Georg Lukács recounted that during the trial of the Hungarian communist Zoltán Szántó and his companions, in which a heavy sentence was expected, he wrote to Thomas Mann and asked him to protest against this terror trial. To this Mann replied that he was well known to believe that writers should not interfere in political issues: for him this was a political trial, with which as a writer he therefore should have nothing to do. Hence he would not protest. In his reply Lukács argued that Mann had recently visited Pilsudski's Poland and given lectures there — wasn't this politics? With this, thought Lukács, "communication was broken off", but he was mistaken. A few days later there came a cable from Thomas Mann with the message: "I have telegrammed Horthy."

This is a typical and particularly good example of a successful value discussion. Lukács proved that there was a *discrepancy* between the value to which his partner was committed and his deeds. Thomas Mann considered this; abstracted from all personal motives, from any feeling of being insulted, from the type of vanity of "quod dixi, dixi", and without hesitation removed the discrepancy. It is unnecessary to go into in detail that a *precondition* for this successful value discussion was a *consensus* in relation to certain *value ideas*, even though the two men gave them a *different meaning*.

In everyday value discussions the *correctness* of values in relation to concrete actions is tested. In "ascending" value discussions *the truth of the correct values* is tested. In philosophical value discussion one *enters with true values*. Here we have to assume that *the value of the partner who takes up a philosophical value discussion with us is equally a true value*, that the values of both of us are related to the same value idea, and that their common validation is *conceivable*.

However, with this we encounter for the second time the *antinomy* of societies based on subordination and superordination. That is, in such societies it is *not even conceivable* that all value interpretations belonging to one and the same value idea *could* be validated; their general observance is *mutually exclusive*. In societies based on subordination and superordination, philosophical value discussion is not generalisable. At the same time every rational being should strive to hold their value discussions at the level of philosophical value discussion. The philosophical nature of value discussion thus imposes on every rational being a *regulative idea*.

Once again we shall leave open the question whether or not this antinomy can be dissolved. We do this because we have now reached one of the most difficult problems in value discussion: *the discussion over values*.

If one value idea confronts another value idea, then the value discussion *always returns to the discussion over values, and thus two worlds confront each other*. When mutually exclusive historical epochs and the social agents who represent them confront each other in fundamental social conflict, then they always have *contradictory value ideas*. If the truth of an idea of value is put into question, then so too is an *entire world epoch* and the social agents who represent it.

When the dominant value ideas of world historical epochs are mutually exclusive, then normally one cannot imagine any value discussion that concerns value ideas occurring between their representatives. Christ and the Grand Inquisitor would not be able to convince each other. The maximum result of such a value discussion would be that the participants realised that they both thought and acted in value rational terms. Yet even in this situation, each of them could only hold their own value to be true, and neither could be convinced of the truth of the other's value. This is really self-evident, since two contradictory and mutually exclusive ideas can hardly be true at the same time, in the same place and in the same relationship. Either one or the other is true: either . . . or. There is an unforgettable description of this in Schiller. However passionately Posa speaks of freedom to the king, he can only achieve one thing, and that is the most that he could: Philip recognises that his opponent acts in value rational terms and that his value "appears" as true to him. But not for a moment will the king recognise this value to be true. If he did this, his world would collapse. Either . . . or.

And yet such an *apparently* hopeless value discussion is of extraordinary importance. The ideal of philosophical value discussion (and of all value discussions which lead up to philosophical value discussion) is certainly at the centre of our concerns; certainly we have claimed that discussions over value ideas are not nearly so frequent as is usually claimed; nonetheless, we do not want to denigrate their historical relevance.

The criteria of philosophical value discussion cannot be applied to value discussions which result from a collision between value ideas, because one cannot imagine the values that here confront each other being validated together in the future. If one looks back to the discussions of the past, then this observation admittedly appears irrelevant. In the past, criteria other than those recommended here were the criteria of the true value. Yet whatever these criteria may have been, it is clear that of two opposing ideas of value, only one could have been true. However, if there are universally valid value ideas, as in the present, their universal validity signifies precisely that no discussion over them is, and can be, conducted. The discussion over ideas is thus restricted to the discussion about the *hierarchy* of universal value ideas.

Discussions over contradictory value ideas do not aim *prim-*

arily at convincing the participants in the discussion. Certainly this could be an aim: indeed one ought to assume that the other is also capable of choosing a new value. Yet such discussions are really aimed at a *"third"*. In discussions over contradictory value ideas, the participants address themselves above all to those who have not yet clarified their values, those who still are open to a reception. Discussion of contradictory values is always performed on the *world stage*. It is the "souls" — the recipients — who decide for the new, who relativise the old. The "losing" value drops out of the list of value ideas; although certainly not necessarily out of the list of values. However, it is henceforth no longer a "leading value". If one wants to hold it to be true, then one must relate it to other valid values, and one must so interpret it that it can be related to other valid values. The idea of value that is in statu nascendi *will be defended by its founders with their own body, they will nourish it with their own blood*, until it raises itself to the level of general validity.

The arrival of a new value idea always brings with it a "regrouping" and a reordering of the value system. The value discussion which flares up around this new value idea makes this reordering explicit and places it on the agenda. One thinks of the arrival of the idea of value "Equality of all before the law". Confronted with this new idea of value, the Enlightenment had to revalue and redefine numerous old values, for example revenge. From then on these old values acquired a *negative* accent, since they contradicted the new values of a universal legal system applying equally to all.

We said that the founders of the emerging idea of value will defend it with their body and nourish it with their blood. Yet this applies — if not always so emphatically — more or less to all values. Value discussion can never be separated from social praxis, from the life of those who participate in the discussion, from their individuality as whole human beings. Such a separation is always only an abstraction. *Deeds are also arguments*; experience and events are also arguments.

If, as a result of their experiences, a person or a group of people develops a feeling of hostility towards the *inherited values* — a feeling that "something is wrong" with these values — then *they are prepared to allow themselves to be convinced in a value discussion.*

Should a value discussion at first end without any result, but one of the discussion partners subsequently experiences something which shakes their trust and their belief in their own values, then the value discussion can lead to a result *after the event*. One convincing experience that events can lead to is: what is happening or has happened to me, and what is happening or has happened to others.

In prison Croesus moans, "Oh Solon, Solon!" — he recognises that in a value discussion in the distant past, which had at the time ended indecisively, Solon's argument had been true. *What Croesus had experienced showed that his interpretation of the value "happiness" could not withstand the test, that Solon had been right all along to claim that nobody could be called happy until they had died.*

In the last scene of Schiller's tragedy, Don Carlos puts the freedom of Flanders above love. This restructuring of his value hierarchy is motivated by things which others had experienced and which others had done: by the king's murder and by Posa's self-sacrifice.

From a *moral* point of view it is *not* all the same whether someone restructures their value hierarchy on the basis of their *own* experience or on the basis of *another's* experience. However, from the point of view of the success of the value discussion, the two cases are equivalent.

The fact that events and experience have an impact on the choice of new values does not however remove the decisive importance of the value discussion itself. When someone is won over *after* the discussion, it is *the arguments* of the value discussion which are still vibrating. Thus in prison Croesus could moan, "Oh Solon, Solon!" which is to say: "In the value discussion between us you were right, now I am convinced."

Everyday value discussions frequently come back to the *particular* motive of the other person: "You only condemn war because you are cowardly" or "Your vanity prevents you from seeing that you are wrong."

In value discussions in which we want to test the truth of our correct values, that is to say, in discussions which develop from everyday value discussions into philosophical value discussions, we can *never* and must *never* refer to the other's particular motives. If this does happen, the value discussion immediately sinks to the level of everyday value discussion. One can indeed assume that the other has particular motives, but one *can never argue that they do*.

In philosophical value discussion one starts from the assumption that both sides are committed to the truth of their own value. A particularistic motive *cannot be assumed*. At the same time *neither* in everyday *nor* in philosophical value discussion is it assumed *that the values which are in debate are not the expression of particular interests or of mutually contradictory social needs, or do not at least show an affinity with these*. Philosophical value discussion is structured as a confrontation between true values. If the value can be deduced from the interest, then a philosophical value discussion is quite simply impossible. If the value can be deduced from needs, or if it is simply an expression of them, then the philosophical value discussion is only an illusion which one can strip off. In this case philosophical value discussion is basically impossible.

If however *the* value can be deduced neither from interests nor from needs, but nonetheless the concrete values do show an affinity to interests or needs, then philosophical value discussion is *in principle possible*. Yet in societies which are based on subordination and superordination, it can only be merely a regulatory function and not a constitutive idea. It is therefore, in other words, *not possible*. Yet philosophical value discussion *should exist*.

Let us now consider whether value discussion is *possible in principle*. Values are primary social facts. Every society is a system of institutions and customs, which presupposes a system which consciously privileges some people and disadvantages others with the help of categories of value orientation. There are only interests in class societies, since they are constituted on a *contradiction of interests*. Here it is enough to mention Marx's ethnological manuscripts, in which, if only in outline, he attempts to show how contradictory interests emerged together with class society. Interest is therefore a secondary social fact, and a primary social fact cannot be deduced from a secondary one.

Just like value, need is a *primary* social fact. A system of needs is constituted through the aid of values, but these are not identical with the system of needs. In societies that are both classless and also stagnant, the system of needs coincides with the value system. In all hitherto existing class societies however, the system of needs that is given in social objectifications is *not* identical with the system of values, and this is also the case for individuals. If values and needs were identical, then *there would be no contradiction between the validity of values and their validation*. At the same time a value can itself become a need. In brief: value cannot be deduced from need. Philosophical value discussion is thus *in principle* possible.

The statement that, as social facts, values cannot be deduced from interests or needs, does not however mean that the concrete values of particular concrete individuals and groups cannot be related to their needs and interests. In every society in which there is a social division of labour, *the place occupied within the social division of labour results in an affinity with certain values and a tendency to reject others*. Affinity is certainly not the same as determination. Indeed, class societies are characterised precisely by heterogeneity in their value system. This implies the *possibility* that one chooses a value (or chooses and interprets one's values) in such a way that the choice precisely does *not* express one's place in the social division of labour. Nonetheless, this affinity will be present in all value discussions in societies based on relationships of subordination and superordination. Yet it can certainly happen that someone takes up the "ideal standpoint" of another social entity, so that their values primarily express their affinity to this entity, without their having become part of it as far as the social division of labour is concerned. And this is particularly true in modern society.

In a society in which there are conflicts of interest, in which needs and their satisfaction stand in an antagonistic relationship, a value discussion in which these contradictions are *not* expressed is completely impossible.

Philosophical value discussion is always a discussion between true values. However, in the case of a confrontation between values which show an affinity with opposing interests, can one assume that all the values which are brought into the discussion are true? In relation to values that manifest an affinity to needs the satisfaction of which is mutually exclusive, can one assume that all these values are true? Once again therefore we pose the question: is philosophical value discussion possible in a society which is based on subordination and superordination?

If one were to reply, "It is impossible", then this amounts to saying: *This world must be the way it is.* If something is to be changed then something has to change. For the creation of a society that is *not* based on relationships of subordination and superordination, there must be people to bring it into existence. That, however, can only be done by people who as equals engage in a philosophical value discussion with each other. One precondition for a world which is not based on the inherited division of labour, for a world in which people control their own social conditions of existence, is that — even if only as an ideal — everyone participates in the formation of ideas of value. Therefore philosophical value discussion *should* be held.

Here a crucial question is raised. Can there be a social entity which has *no interests* and which serves as an *orientative* idea in value discussion? Interests are constituted in conflicts of interest. Is there a social entity which has no conflicts of interest with any other social entity?

One such entity does exist: *humankind*. Considered as a whole, humankind does not have any interests, *for there is no entity which would have opposing interests to it*. Values therefore which relate to the value "humankind" are *not* the expression of an affinity with any interests. However, humanity is a *not a real community*, but rather an *idea of value*, the highest idea of value of the *social entity*. Since however it is not a real community, *every concrete interpretation of this idea — with* whatever meaning we may give it, however we may want to adhere to it — will always express an affinity with what is, with a particular entity, stratum, class or community.

What is to be done? Our values, which manifest an affinity with the needs and interests of particular groupings, are those same values which claim universal validity as interpretations of the idea of value. That is to say, value discussions contain *an ideological moment*. Worse still: for so long as there exists an inherited division of labour which constitutes and expresses relationships of subordination and superordination, the ideological moment in value discussions *cannot be avoided*.

At the same time however, *philosophical value discussion must not be of an ideological character*. In philosophical value discussion *the particular must not be put forward as the universal*. That is, as long as one's own value interpretation — one's own proposal for the realisation of universally valid values — is put forward as the only possible true value interpretation, then we cannot assume that the value of the partner who confronts us in the value discussion is equally true. If a value that expresses an affinity with the interests or the system of needs of a particular group, appears as *the* universal and *the* true in a value discussion, then our value interpretation has an ideological character and hence *no philosophical value discussion can be held*.

REASON AND THE CHALLENGE TO IDEOLOGY

Once again — and in yet another context — we are confronted with the *antinomy*. Philosophical value discussion is not possible in societies based on relationships of subordination and superordination, yet in these societies a philosophical value discussion should occur. In addition, philosophical value discussion must not be a merely regulative idea, but also has to be a constitutive one. If it were not, then society based on relationships of subordination and superordination *would be permanent*.

If however we recall the features of the antinomy, then it

emerges that it has two "levels". At one level the antinomy cannot be removed; at the other it is completely possible to remove it. If however the antinomy is removed at this second level, then this can lead to removing the antinomy itself.

What then are these two levels?

The first aspect of the antinomy was that in a society which is based on relationships of subordination and superordination, philosophical value discussion is not generalisable, yet according to the norm of philosophy, every rational being *ought* to participate in philosophical value discussion. The second aspect was that in societies based on relationships of subordination and superordination, a philosophical value discussion is not possible, yet if this society is to abolished, then philosophical value discussion should be a constitutive idea. In what follows I would like to undertake an attempt to dissolve this antinomy in practice. This is only conceivable at the *second level* of the antinomy.

It was said that humankind is a social entity that cannot be thought of within "conflicts of interest". However, from this it follows that a philosophical value discussion is only possible between discussion partners who relate *all* their values to humankind as *the* universal entity. *No philosophical value discussion can be held* between partners for one of whom humankind counts as the highest social entity, while for the other a particular entity has a higher place than humankind.

If in a value discussion every single partner holds humankind to be the highest social entity, then the discussion can reach a philosophical level. This can be so, even though each partner expresses their values and their proposals in the form of concrete and mutually divergent values which reveal an affinity to their *own particular* entity, stratum, class, etc. However, there are several preconditions for such a discussion.

Between representatives of values which are *related to* humankind and which display an affinity with concrete social entities, a philosophical value discussion is *only then possible* when it is possible to *conceive* the particular values being validated simultaneously. This can be possible, *even when the values are in fact mutually opposed to each other* for they cannot be observed simultaneously under present circumstances. If the simultaneous validation of the values *cannot even be thought*, then *no* philosophical value discussion can occur between the opponents.

For example, A may say, "The highest concern of humanity is the maintenance and further development of European culture", while B may say, "The highest concern of humanity is the development of the Third World". These two evaluative statements may at the moment demand different actions, even conflicting ones, if their value component is to be observed. Certainly this contradiction is also reflected in the interpretation of concrete values such as "personality" or "equality". Nonetheless it is clear that the simultaneous achievement of the two evaluated goals is *conceivable*: the maintenance and development of European culture is *conceivable* together with the development of the Third World. *A philosophical value discussion* is therefore *possible* between the representatives of these two interpretations.

The second precondition is that philosophical value discussion can only occur when both partners *are clear* that their values and their value interpretations show an affinity with a concrete social entity (hence to a class, stratum, nation, culture, etc). They must always be conscious of this affinity if they are not to *mislead themselves about the ideological aspect of their values*. Every discussion partner has the right *also* to point out the particular affinities of the values and value interpretations of the other, but only when they do the same in relation to their own values. A discussion partner's task is therefore consciously and continually to purge their own value interpretation *of ideological aspects*.

Admittedly the dissolution of ideology can never be complete. However, it must be achieved to a certain extent if philosophical value discussion is even to occur at all. The point that must be reached is the recognition of the fact that, in so far as they meet the criterion of true value (see above), the values of the other discussion partner are also *true values*.

Finally, the third precondition of philosophical value discussion is that people accept philosophical value discussion as a regulative idea. They therefore have to recognise that *all people are equally rational beings* and that *philosophical value discussion is generalisable. They must therefore desire the abolition of society based on relationships of subordination and superordination. Those people who want to maintain such a form of society are incapable of holding a philosophical value discussion either amongst themselves or with those who do not share their beliefs.*

If — to return to the quotation from Kant — people merely want to continue what has hitherto existed, if they do not recognise the guidance of the practical idea of the highest good either in theory building or in action, if they do not accept the idea of philosophical value discussion, then they will not need any philosophical value discussion either. Such people can merely isolate facts from values, that is to say, they can allow themselves to be guided by everyday values; they can merely claim that value judgements cannot be "true", they can merely announce that value choice is irrational, instead of philosophy they can content themselves with the "scandal of philosophy".

However, if people want to change things so that things should be changed, if they want every rational being to participate in the determination of human values, then they have here and now to carry out their value discusssions at the level of philosophical value discussion. In a society which is based on relationships of subordination and superordination philosophical value discussion cannot be generalised. If it could be generalised, then this would be a sign that society was no longer based on relationships of subordination and superordination. Those however who want such a society to cease to exist ought now already be striving to carry out their value discussions at a philosophical level.

For such people their highest reference point therefore has to be humankind. Their values show an affinity with their own — concrete — social reality, but they have to strive to formulate their values so that one can imagine them being validated together with those values which show an affinity with other social entities. The only precondition is that, in line with the norm of value discussion, all these values develop from the will to overcome relationships of subordination and superordination.

Such people must therefore always be conscious of the ideological aspect of their own value interpretation; they have to make clear to themselves with which social entity their value interpretation has an affinity. They cannot posit their own value interpretation as the *only* true value interpretation. They have to make clear to themselves that the universal validity of their own value and the universal validity of the values which are in debate are not mutually exclusive — so long as there is a consensus in relation to the universal ideas of value and so long as the simultaneous validation of the two values is conceivable. In fact, one only enters into a philosophical value discussion when one assumes that the value in debate is true. Philosophical value discussion actually is a value discussion amongst equals, in which every participant recognises and values the others as representatives of humankind. In philosophical discussion Kant's demand that one should respect humanity in every person has to become unconditionally valid.

We have seen that a philosophical discussion between true values is a genuine discussion. Even in a discussion of true values it is possible for one participant to convince the other. However, in this sort of discussion someone is convinced not by recognising that a true value is untrue, but by the representatives of one value, which displays an affinity with the needs of one social group, seeing that the needs of another group are more important, in other words, are primary. Therefore those who have been convinced do not give up their own values, but instead, whether for a particular case, a particular time or a particular situation, they allow values which express an affinity with another need to have preference. Those however to whom this preference has been conceded will never question that the value which shows an affinity to another social context is itself also true, and in another case and in another situation they will ensure that its realisation is given the priority. This type of value discussion can be successful precisely because the simultaneous validation of the different values is conceivable. Therefore we can say that in philosophical value discussion all that happens is that the discussion partners consciously accept the *dilemma of morality*, the suitability of the observance of the value to the particular situation or person. With this they do not make any claim that the action is universally valid, but they do make such a claim for the value which guides all the actions. After all, the dilemma of morality occurs precisely when there is a collision between values and, depending on the concrete situation, the acting person and the subject or object of the action: the observance of one value has to be given priority, without disclaiming the universal validity of the other value. In every value discussion its conclusion (and the form and manner of its conclusion) is *the personal responsibility of all the participants* — it is their personal responsibility as rational beings; for every conclusion to every philosophical value discussion everyone has to take personal responsibility.

It is not a criterion of value rationality that the evaluated goals will actually be achieved: for this there is *no guarantee*. The fact that we want a free association of people, the fact that for us philosophical value discussion *ought to become an idea of value*, is still no guarantee that this will also *happen*. But because we want it, we *should* also assume that it will happen. If it is to happen, we have to uphold the rationality of our value, and in such a way that we here and now bring into existence communities within which philosophical value discussion is possible.

It was however claimed that in a society based on relationships of subordination and superordination philosophical value discussion is not possible. And that is indeed the case. It is easy to put forward a model, but one must also recognise that anyone who, precisely at the moment when it is difficult to act and difficult to decide, carries out an action or takes a decision in an action, is inclined to make *the only true value* that value which shows an affinity with their *own* social reality, and in general tends *not* to uncover the ideological element in their own value. They are all the less likely to do this because it is *easier* to win people to an action if one presents one's own value as the single true value. And nonetheless philosophical value discussion ought to be held. For what is easy, can be *all too easy*: it can happen that it leads us *somewhere else* than where we want to go.

Society will be based on relationships of subordination and superordination for as long as philosophical value discussion *cannot* be generalised. To make our own values the "only true" values is the easy way, but it does not lead us where we want to go. This is not the sort of action which will lead our own community up to the level of philosophical value discussion, since it does not lead towards overcoming relationships based on subordination and superordination.

Philosophical value discussion therefore ought to be a *constitutive* idea. In our value discussions we have to strive to move at the level of philosophical value discussion. *Even when we cannot achieve this, we must always maintain the will to achieve it.* The challenge of philosophy ought to be addressed to everyone, and therefore philosophy ought every day to address *more people* with its "Consider how you ought to think, consider how you ought to live, consider how you ought to act". The "introduction to philosophy" ought to address each person, and philosophy ought therefore to appeal to ever more people with its call: "Come, let us think together, let us seek the truth together." This is a hard and taxing path. Yet if it is not taken, then society based on relationships of subordination and superordination cannot be left behind.

Philosophy is addressed to the person who seeks the truth. Philosophy constitutes the ideal of the good, the true and the beautiful; it constitutes them for all those who seek the truth. Philosophy is needed by all those who want to think, live and act differently from how they have thought, lived and acted up to now.

There is however more than one way in which one can respond to the challenge of philosophy. The recipient of philosophy can also respond to this challenge as a mere individual, in that from now on they think, live, and act differently from before. In this case the relationship to all rational beings is only a *hypothetical* relation. This however is an exceptional situation. Philosophers form "schools" and recipients too form schools. Mostly they create a small community of equals, a "congregation" which lives, thinks and acts at the level of what ought to be. In this case the relation to all reasonable beings is both *hypothetical and actual* at the same time. Within the particular community the recipients of philosophy face each other as equally reasonable beings. *With this they give the world a norm, but no world to the norm.*

Ever since the idea emerged that people choose and constitute their values themselves, ever since in other words the rigid value hierarchies collapsed and concrete values were relativised, certain abstract values were raised to the level of universally valid value ideas. Since the appearance on the world stage of *sentimental philosophy* it has hardly been possible to follow just these two paths. The crisis of philosophy, the starting point of these considerations, was not least the reaction to this situation. The first great sentimental philosophers, above all Kant and Fichte, were quite conscious of this change. In Kant the turning point is very plain: while before the French Revolution the main tendency of his philosophy was to give the world norms (*The Critique of Practical Reason*), after the Revolution he is more and more concerned to think systematically through to the end how a world can be created for the norm (*Religion, The Metaphysic of Morals*). In Marx this thought "reaches its self-consciousness": *one can only give the world a norm, if one also gives a world to the norm.*

The philosophy of the nineteenth century did not want to give the norm a world, and thus ceased to give the world a norm. It is this which one has since termed "positivism", it is this that is the scandal of philosophy. For there is no philosophy without the ideal of the highest good, there is no original philosophy which has not wanted to give the world a norm. *Today* however, to give the world a norm means to give a world to the norm: *today* there is no other way. It is possible that tomorrow it will again be different, but this tomorrow is still far away. Certainly up to now the philosophers have not only explained the world, but today it really is a question of changing it.

Philosophy is obviously not a god: alone it cannot change the world. To the extent that it presents the world with a norm which can give the norm a world, it can however be part of a praxis that changes the world. All those people who want to end society based on relationships of subordination and superordination today need philosophy. They need norms and ideals which give a perspective from which they can change the world. Philosophical value discussion is itself such an ideal: to put it precisely, it is the ideal of *democratic* value discussion and opinion formation. A norm *ought* to be given to the world, so that a world *can* be created for the norm.

I do not claim to have said that today there is only a need for a radical philosophy. I merely claim that there are radical needs which today *cannot be explicated at all* without philosophy.

5

Radical Philosophy and Radical Needs

Philosophy is homesickness, said Novalis. All sentimental philosophy is homesickness, the longing for a world in which philosophy is at home. As long as philosophy wants to give a norm to the world, it finds itself at home in morality and in comprehension. So long as it wants to give a world to the norm, then its homesickness means: "*I want the world to be a home for humanity.*" A world in which humanity is at home is the end of philosophy's odyssey, for in such a world philosophy is at home. Philosophy can only be transcended, so Marx argued, when it is realised. And doubtless this applies to sentimental philosophy and to its fulfilment, radical philosophy.

Philosophy is the demiurge. Philosophy demands that the world becomes a home for humanity, but merely demanding this will not make it happen. *The Ought of philosophy has to become the Will of human beings*, so that one day it can be said: it did happen. Radical philosophy has to become the philosophy of radical movements, it has to "penetrate the masses", it has to "become a material force", so that one day it can be said: it did happen.

Hence in order to say something about radical philosophy, we have first to consider radicalism itself.

REIFIED NEEDS AND THE CRITIQUE OF DOMINATION

By radicalism I understand above all a total critique of society — of a society which rests on relationships of subordination and superordination and on the "natural division of labour". Radical actors are those who, having turned away from bourgeois forms of life and decided in favour of another form of life, also formulate and articulate their justification for this rejection and for this redefinition. Furthermore, radical actors act according to new value interpretations which result from this fundamental decision.

I differentiate between two main types of radicalism: *right-wing radicalism* and *left-wing radicalism*. Between the two I see a *structural* difference, which is *relatively independent* of what *concrete ideology* a radical group has appropriated for itself.

For me, right-wing radicalism includes all movements which do not regard humanity as the highest social value. Someone can only be a left-wing radical if for them humanity is the highest idea of value. Further, I characterise as right-wing radicals all those who reject *even only one* of the value-ideas that today have universal validity. Someone can only be a left-wing radical if they accept all the value-ideas that today have universal validity. Finally, I define as right-wing radicals all those *who do not accept the norm of philosophical value discussion*; all those who *are not prepared* consciously to reflect on the ideological nature of their values; all those who are not prepared to recognise that values with an affinity to other groups or societies can also be true. From this results, vice versa, the main criterion of left-wing radicalism: the assumption that all people are equally reasonable beings, the desire that values should be determined by everyone in collective and rational discussion, the striving for a discussion of true values. Thus left-wing radicalism will always retain an aspect of *enlightenment*. Without temporising, left-wing radicalism attempts to make everyone conscious of their *right* and their *duty* to *think for themselves*.

Right-wing radicalism can participate in the everyday value discussions of the time. However, because of its structure it does not contribute to philosophical value discussion. The standard of its arguments necessarily includes the non-rational arguments of everyday value discussion: respect for authority, tracing back discussion partners' arguments to particular interests, slandering, the privileging of *belief* over *conviction*.

Right-wing radicalism is *elitist*. Even when it mobilises the masses with its fanaticism, it remains elitist, since for it "the masses" are not the sum of independent and thinking personalities who participate in the determination of values, but rather a manipulated mass, *not a subject, but an object*. Left-wing radicalism is always *democratic*. It is democratic even when it is isolated and comprises very few people. Yet left-wing radical movements also have a painfully *aristocratic* aspect: they ascribe to every person abilities and values of which the majority of men and women are either ignorant or unconscious. Since, as we know, in societies based on relationships of subordination and superordination philosophical value discussion cannot be generalised, the democracy of left-wing radicalism can never completely overcome its own aristocratic element — for as soon as philosophical value discussion is actually generalised, then radical philosophy loses its relevance. There is however something that every democratic left-wing movement should strive for: to win more and more people for philosophical value discussion and for discussion which clarifies values; it has to try to make more and more subjects conscious of their nature as subjects. In brief, it has to strive for the permanent *relativisation* of its own aristocratic aspect.

We know that this is a tiring and taxing path. Yet it is the only path by which a society of free human beings can be reached; it is the only way the world can actually be made a home for human beings. Right-wing radicalism certainly subjects society as based on relationships of subordination and superordination to a total critique. It also wants to overcome the form of life that goes with these relationships. Yet it can put forward nothing to replace them, apart from new relationships of subordination and superordination; it can do nothing more than reproduce the old mess in another form, for society which is based on relationships of subordination and superordination cannot be overcome through a new structure of subordination and superordination. If things really are to be changed, then things must be changed, not least in precisely the *relationships between people*. To be radical, said

Marx, means to go to the root of things. And, he added, the root of things is human beings themselves.

It was said that philosophy involves enlightenment, and that every philosophy is — in its structure — democratic. It was said that the challenge of philosophy, "Come, let us think together, let us seek the truth together", is addressed to everyone, for philosophy assumes that all people are equally rational beings. It was said that philosophy appeals to the understanding and not to the belief of reasonable people. It was said that philosophy recognises no *other* authority than human reason. For all these reasons, only left-wing radicalism can have a philosophy, never right-wing radicalism.

Without any doubt Marx is the philosophical master of left-wing radicalism. This certainly does not mean that all left-wing radical movements start from Marx, or that all radical philosophers of our time are recipients of Marx. There are numerous left-radical movements which are not linked to Marx. It is possible that they have no philosophy whatsoever, although their efforts do express their need for a radical philosophy. One should mention here radical Christianity, or the movement which I term a "radicalism of the feelings" — the movement or the movements which strive for a new communual form of life — and one can also point to the growing feminist movements. In addition there are many left-orientated philosophies which are completely unconnected in any way to Marx's philosophical conception and its tradition. Yet despite all these qualifications, we must however accept that Marx's philosophy is the only one *canonised* by left-radical movements. What is true for all other philosophy is certainly also true for Marx's: we understand it misunderstandingly and Marx, like every philosopher, can be *differently* understood. Equally, in the existing understanding misunderstanding of his philosophy we cannot lay down any rigid boundaries to separate misunderstanding as understanding from misunderstanding misunderstanding. Excluding simple mistakes and ignorance, there is only one single general criterion to separate understanding misunderstanding from straightforward misunderstanding. It is the same as for every philosophy and every work of art: if the interpreter changes or reverses the value hierarchy, then one is clearly dealing with a mere misunderstanding. However, in so far as the different interpreters uphold the value hierarchy of Marx's philosophy, then we have to consider every misunderstanding understanding of this philosophy as an *equally true understanding*.

We know that every value choice and every value interpretation reveals an affinity with certain social classes, strata and movements, or with their interests and needs. The choice of a philosophy and the form and manner in which it is understood also expresses this affinity. Every radicalism — including the philosophy of left-wing radicalism — shows in its interpretation of ideas of value, in its hierarchies of values, in its presentation of new ideas of value and in its construction of corresponding theories, as well as its praxis, an affinity with *radical needs*, or with the movements, classes and groups which feel, interpret, and formulate these needs.

We characterise as radical needs all needs which arise within a society based on relationships of subordination and superordination, but which *cannot be satisfied* within such a society. These are the needs which can only be satisfied if this society is *transcended*. There are innumerable radical needs, because there are innumerable interpretations of needs which cannot be satisfied within a society based on relationships of subordination and superordination.

A unitary humanity as a reality and not merely as an idea, as a community of the unity of mutually understanding and mutually supporting different forms of life, which all continually remove conflicts of interest between them: that is a radical need. It exists as a need, but it cannot be satisfied within a society constituted by relationships of subordination and superordination and conflicts of interest, within a society of which the dynamic is determined by conflicts of interest.

The developed human personality is one which has expanded its ability for enjoyment, and as such it has a multitude of qualitative needs. The need exists to create the possibility that *every person* can become such a personality. This is a radical need, because it cannot be satisfied within societies based on relationships of subordination and superordination.

I would like to enumerate some further radical needs, without attempting to achieve exhaustiveness. People's wish to determine through rational discussion the development of society and its content, direction and values — that is a radical need. The generalisation of freely chosen communities is a radical need. Equality between people in interpersonal relationships and the elimination of social domination — that is equally a radical need. Reducing across the whole of society the discrepancy between the pressure of socially necessary work and the emptiness of free time — that too is a radical need. The abolition of war and of armaments is a radical need. Today too, more and more people demand that hunger and suffering be removed from the world and the ecological catastrophe be averted. Even the wish to iron out the discrepancy between high culture and mass culture is a radical need. None of the needs which have been listed here can be satisfied within a society based on relationships of subordination and superordination — hence they are all radical needs.

Left-wing radical movements and their philosophical interpretations all have an affinity with radical needs, but not necessarily *to the same ones*. Values which have an affinity with different radical needs can even be mutually contradictory when one attempts to validate them here and now. That is to say, actions guided by different values can aim at diverging, even contradictory, goals, while the theories guided by different values deviate from one another. Radical needs are however needs which one can imagine being satisfied simultaneously. It is even our duty to think how they could be satisfied simultaneously within a society which were *not* to be based on relationships of subordination and superordination. A value discussion is therefore *possible* between values which have an affinity with different radical needs. Everyone who works out their values on the basis of an affinity with particular radical needs, therefore has the *duty* to elevate their value discussions to the level of a philosophical value discussion.

Radical philosophy, the philosophy of Karl Marx, can be understandingly misunderstood in many different ways. The different understanding misunderstandings express an affinity with different radical needs. It is therefore the duty of every recipient of Marx to carry out a philosophical value discussion with the other recipients of Marx. In other words, they must recognise that the other person's understanding misunderstanding is just as *true* as their own understanding misunderstanding. At the same time — and precisely for this reason — they have to make clear to themselves with what radical needs their own interpretation has an affinity, or with which need it has the greatest affinity. Equally, it is their duty to carry out a philosophical discussion with *all* those who express their own affinity with particular radical needs with the help of another conceptual schema.

I would like to apply to myself the demands which I have formulated. I understand myself as a recipient of Marx's philosophy. I am quite clear that my understanding — like every understanding — is simultaneously a misunderstanding. In my interpretation of Marxist philosophy I bring out into the open my affinity with all radical movements which express the need for a community of free people and for the communal determination of values. These are movements for the creation of new forms of life and of self-management. I am well aware that these radical needs are *Euro-centric*. Since I relate my values to the whole of humanity as the highest entity, I obviously want these values to become valid for the whole of humanity. However, at the same time I also know that there are countless other radical needs, and that the values which these express have *just as great* a claim to universal validity. Therefore I recognise as *true* all values and theories which express an affinity with other radical needs. I cannot imagine my own values being realised without in reality all other radical needs also being satisfied. I recognise as true all the understanding misunderstandings of Marxist philosophy which may well deviate from my own, but which nonetheless do not disturb the value hierarchy of this philosophy. At the same time I recognise as true all values with an affinity with left-radical movements which are expressed in *other* conceptual schemas.

Obviously, the statement that I recognise as true a value within a conceptual schema which differs from my own does not mean that I also recognise all the conceptual schemata as true. If for example a conceptual schema has recourse to the hereafter, then I do not recognise it as true, for in my understanding transcendence lies beyond the boundaries of human knowledge: the claims made about it can therefore be neither true nor false. This does not alter the fact that it is possible to find true values within a transcendental conceptual schema.

If a conceptual schema *asserts* true values wihout ordering and justifying them with rational arguments, I do not recognise the theoretical concept as true, even when I do accept the explicit value within it as true. At the same time, if a theoretical concept differs from mine and is rooted in another theoretical tradition, but nonetheless is able to rank and justify the true values within it, I *always* recognise it as true.

THE RATIONAL UTOPIA

Like every philosophy, radical philosophy constitutes itself from the tension between what is and what ought to be, between appearance and essence, between opinion and knowledge. Like every philosophy, it understands what is on the basis of its definition of what ought to be. Like every philosophy, it also wishes to deduce what ought to be from what is — the "what is" that it has constructed on the basis of what ought to be. Like every philosophy, it generalises the value judgement "Not this but that is good" into a concrete and universal ideal. Like every philosophy, it is also a rational utopia. Like every philosophy, it commits itself to "ens perfectissimum, ens realissimum". It produces and reproduces the commitment of every philosophy: sub specie aeternitatis, écrasez l'infâme!

I do not wish to analyse here Marxist philosophy, since I have done that in another context.[23] I shall limit myself to merely a few remarks.

Marx's "what ought to be", his rational utopia, is communism, the society of associated producers in which alienation — the discrepancy between the individual and the human species — is overcome. For Marx the level of appearance is the fetishised character of capitalism, in which essential human relationships appear as relationships among things. Mere opinion originates from fetishism in theory construction, as for example in vulgar economy, while knowledge proceeds from theoretical production concerning the essence. One can reach true knowledge from two standpoints: from the standpoint of bourgeois society or from the standpoint of humanity as a social entity, the standpoint of rational utopia. The latter is knowledge constituted through true value, it is a unity of the good and the true. Marx however deduces what ought to be from two mutually contradictory conceptions. In the first, what ought to be has to be deduced from what is through the category of necessity; in the second, human praxis — human action — mediates between what is and what ought to be. Quite consciously I accept the second solution. The value judgement which serves as a starting point, "Not this is good, not this is true, but that is good, that is true", is subjected by Marx to a total critique: the total critique of *every* society based on relationships of subordination and superordination. The critique of political economy is at the same time a total critique of one form of life from the point of view of a new form of life. The rational utopia is at the same time *true* history in opposition to hitherto existing history. It is also the realisation of the species, the end of the odyssey of historically developed being, its "homecoming" to a home where human beings become what they truly are. If this is to be realised, the present must perish, for this is how Marx interprets Hegel's dialectic that that *which is no longer rational*, must perish: écrasez l'infâme!

To understand Marx's work as a *rational utopia* means nothing other than to understand it as *philosophy*. It cannot however be denied that Marx himself understood his work above all as *science*: Engels therefore speaks of the development of socialism from utopia to science. The emphasis on science is relevant both historically and to the essential claim of Marxist philosophy. The historical relevance can be briefly summarised by saying that Marx and Engels lived in the century of positivism; this positivism shaped their theory, or at least its interpretation. With Engels, in my opinion, positivism left its traces within the theory itself, whereas with Marx it is confined to the interpretation. In that period the idea of the true was so much seen as part of science that a true theory had to be described as "science". Yet there is a still more important aspect. We will see later that radical philosophy involves an application of its own philosophy in social theory. With Marx this application was — when one considers his work as a whole — doubtless dominant. Yet to put a philosophy into relationship with social science always presupposes the philosophical structuring of the social facts of a particular concrete epoch. Hence the practical relevance of a social science (that is, its relevance in the definition and formulation of the strategy of social action) is necessarily time-bound. In no way was Marx's social science an exception. A critique of it from the point of view of the understanding and the interpretation of the rather different facts, problems and conflicts of present-day society therefore appears to us neither superfluous nor irrelevant. However we do claim that this critique does not undermine Marx's *philosophical* conception. Hence Marx's philosophical conception can be applied in a different social theory which is suitable to the present. I am certainly not claiming that Marx's philosophy as a rational utopia is above criticism. Every philosophy can be criticised. I am merely claiming that the critique of his social theory does *not inherently* involve a critique of his philosophy, and that one can falsify his philosophy as little as one can falsify any other philosophy. His philosophy lives and is alive *as long as there are people who turn to it*. In what follows we therefore consider it justified to discuss Marx as a philosopher, and only as a philosopher.

Up to now we have shown to what a broad extent all the justifications for philosophy also apply to Marx's philosophy. Now however we have to answer a different question, namely why this philosophy is radical. Doubtless radical philosophy is a continuation of the principles and concerns of sentimental philosophy. It is certainly no accident Marx is so frequently interpreted from the point of view of Kant, Fichte, Hegel, Feuerbach, or the romantics, but never from that of Spinoza, Descartes, Leibniz or Locke. Yet Marxian radical philosophy is characterised by factors which are present in no other sentimental philosophy. Taken by themselves, none of these aspects is only characteristic of radical philosophy, but radical philosophy is the only one that is shaped by all of them taken together.

What then are these characteristics?

Marx placed his rational utopia in *humanity's immanent future*. For him this immanent future as a form of life is in *opposition* to the capitalist form of life, which merely means that the route from one to the other is only conceivable as *a revolution of the entire society*. He considered the carrier of such a revolution to be those people *who have radical needs: he assumed that the needs of the working class are such radical needs. He saw the task of philosophy as mediating between the radical movements and the radical utopia.* However, if people are to carry out such a revolution, then they not only need a radical utopia, but also a *recognition of the possibilities* — and always of the concrete social possibilities within which they are acting. One organic and inherent aspect of radical philosophy is therefore the development of its *own social theory*. This theory has to be confronted with those social theories constituted "from the view-point of bourgeois society" and, mediated by this confrontation, with bourgeois society itself.

This last aspect has already been formulated as a norm by Kant: ". . .everything is lost, when the empirical and therefore accidental conditions for the application of the law become conditions of the law itself, and so a praxis which is calculated on the basis of what *previous experience* showed to be the probable outcome is allowed to dominate theory that exists as an end in itself." Kant's demand is clearly part of the social theory of radical philosophy. It structures the empirical and therefore accidental conditions from the point of view of the law of the radical utopia, since it searches for the possibilities of a radical utopia and the conditions in which it can be realised. It does not allow the rational utopia to depend on those empirical facts to which Kant refers. A philosophy can only be termed radical if it does not just formulate this as a norm, but also *carries it out*. A radical philosophy which does not apply its own values in social theory, which does not take upon itself the task of considering and thematising the empirical conditions for the realisation of the rational utopia, such a philosophy is equally not a radical philosophy. Radical philosophy too has its *dilemma*, the resolution of which is at the same time a *duty* which the world has imposed on it: it cannot be a radical philosophy, if it is *only* a philosophy. It also therefore has to be a social theory, a critical social theory.

It was not easy for me to formulate this "only": I am after all writing a confession to philosophy. Can one confess love to someone whom one loves and then say to them, they should not "only" be what they are? Can one say of an objectification that formulates the highest good, that it should not "only" do that? Can one say "only" of something which in itself and for itself occupies the highest rank?

Times will only be happy again when a philosophy exists to which one cannot apply this little word "only"! But who would claim that we live in happy times? We live in a time in which the suffering imposed by people on other people is immeasurable, in which every other norm must be related to the imperative "An end must be put to this misery." A philosophy that is "only" philosophy has no ears to hear the cries of human suffering. One *ought* to help and one *ought* to see how and where one can help. Radical philosophy must not forget its rational utopia for a single moment, it has to remain philosophy, for when it does not, it will no longer be capable of subsuming the accidental facts under the theory constituted by universal values. Yet it cannot remain "only" a philosophy, for it is its task to subsume the empirical facts under the theory. Radical philosophy must never fail in this task, for it has to put forward *recommendations* for help and relief everywhere and in every situation. "Never" here means — for as long as society based on relationships of subordination and superordination continues to exist.

Philosophy demands: "Consider how you should think.

Consider how you should live. Consider how you should act."
Where and how can radical philosophy achieve this, where
and how ought it to achieve this?

In order to answer these questions we must recall what was
originally said of the relationship between complete and partial reception. In bourgeois society the complete and the partial types of reception stand in an inverted relationship to each
other. More and more obstacles develop to complete reception, while the types of partial reception breed and multiply.
Partial reception is thus an expression of the need for philosophy in a time in which, as a result of specialisation, complete
reception becomes more and more difficult. The path which
leads from the partial to the general has been broken. It is the
duty of radical philosophy to make this path passable again. It
is its duty to turn to those who show by their partial reception
their claim to philosophy; it is however its duty to always
satisfy the need for partial reception from the viewpoint of the
totality of philosophy and its rational utopia. Only thus will it
be able to reach all those who seek the truth. Only thus will it
be able to guide partial recipients to a complete reception.
However, radical philosophers do not just have to construct
the rational utopia which incorporates in the form of concrete
and universal ideals philosophy's demand, "Consider how you
should think, consider how you should act, consider how you
should live." They also have to develop an answer point for
point to the distinct questions posed by all three demands and
an answer to the needs and their satisfaction which all three
special demands involve.

On the basis of all this, I see the fundamental tasks of
radical philosophy as follows:

(a)   It has to take upon itself what is in the strict sense of the
word its philosophical task. By generalising the value judgement "Not this, but that is true" it has to develop ideals which
embody the rational utopia. This does not mean an exhaustive
and detailed description of a future society, for we can hardly
know anything concrete of the "society of the future". The
rational utopia is always conceived for the *present*, its ideals
show the — relative — aim in the direction of which one

should progress in the present, and the aim for which one should act in the present. This aim is a value aim, the corresponding action is therefore value rational; only the aim of purposive rational action is present from the start in people's heads. Radical philosophy has to take the risk of *raising* certain given values to the status of value ideas. In the light of these value ideas, radical philosophy has to criticise society which rests on relationships of subordination and superordination: it has to put in place of its form of life a new form of life. Its critique has to be total; it has to develop its utopia in such a way that it has to be achieved by a total *social* revolution.

(b) Radical philosophy has to satisfy the need expressed in the statement: "Consider how you should think." In this connection too, radical philosophers have to be partial recipients of their own philosophies. Their ideal of a rational utopia requires them to take upon themselves the task of developing a social theory in three different areas. However, a common aspect of all three areas is that they all involve questions as to the *possibility* of the radical utopia. In relation to the possibilties of what it wants, philosophy poses no questions: it always assumes that one can do what one ought to do. Nonetheless, it is the duty of radical philosophers to examine *whether* what ought to be is possible, and — more importantly — *how* it is possible.

(ba) Radical philosophy has to *raise anthropological issues*. Philosophy constructs its system from the ideal of humanity, from the ideal of the species. Radical philosophy however has to answer the question whether empirical human beings and empirical humanity are suited to realise the ideal of the radical utopia. For radical needs — and it is to them that radical philosophy shows an affinity — are the interpreted needs of only a minority of empirical humanity. Radical philosophy therefore has to ask whether it is possible to generalise these needs. It has to investigate not the ideal of the species, but rather *the social nature of human beings* and their inherent possibilities. It is necessary to counterpoise a new anthropology to the anthropology of Hobbes.

(bb) Radical philosophy has to be a *critical social theory*. It has to consider *contemporary* processes of social life and within these it particularly has to consider all conflict situations. It has to investigate *if* and how, starting from these concrete conflict situations, the radical utopia can be reached. It has to consider economic and political relationships, nationality conflicts, classes and strata, the forms of manipulation, work and working conditions, education and distribution, law, ideology, etc. After each concrete analysis it has to put forward concrete proposals, proposals which are realisable and which *at the same time* are formulated from the perspective of the values of the rational utopia. It therefore has to integrate itself into the creation of *programmes of reform*.

(bc)   Since radical philosophy is a philosophy with historical consciousness, it also has to investigate the *origin* of the social structure of today. Indeed, there can be no answer to the question of possibility without some consideration of history. Radical philosophy has to explain how social categories can be both historical and universal. Within this, and without giving up its claim that its ideals are universally valid, radical philosophy has to *reflect historically on itself*. However, the precondition for this is that the problem of the unity of the historicity and the universality of social categories is resolved by uncovering the historicity of contemporary social structure.

(c)   Like every other philosophy, radical philosophy puts forward a form of life. It says to its complete recipients: "Live your life according to your philosophy!" Yet radical philosophy also has to give a distinct answer to the question "How should one live?" It has to give an answer to the partial recipients of philosophy and satisfy their needs; starting from their choice of a form of life, it has to lead them up to the complete reception of philosophy. Radical philosophy therefore cannot content itself with advice as to how one should live. It also has to address those who ask how *can* one live — here and now? It is therefore one of its duties to develop, starting from the point of view of what ought to be, a statement about what is possible. Radical philosophy also has to be a philosophy of life (*Lebensphilosophie*). Quite clearly, radical philosophy cannot exclude the need of contemporary human beings for an answer to the question "How should one live?"

If purposive rational orientation expands in the sphere of value rationality (the sphere of social communication and interaction) then, to the extent they are not completely subordinated to the satisfaction of purely quantitative needs, people's lives start to lose sense and meaning. However, if they are completely subordinated to purely quantitative needs, then they lose any sense and meaning whatsoever. In the current phase of the bourgeois epoch the individual is becoming more and more "atomised" and feels more and more isolated. Simultaneously this same individual is subjected to conformist role expectations, and this duality leads to the disintegration of the personality. In this situation people suffer. Customary norms become looser; irrational violence, controlled by no social norm whatsoever, spreads. Isolation, the disintegration of the personality, violence — all create permanent fear.

However, the disintegrated personality, at the mercy of its drives and the violence of others, nonetheless resists the deterioration of its own condition. It feels that it ought to give life meaning, but it cannot. The personality resists. It even resists through forms of unconscious rejection, such as neuroses and the self-forgetfulness induced by the permanent "high" of drugs. Yet it also resists consciously: in the movements of radical feelings. These movements are searching for a new form of life, a form of life which will give life meaning.

Radical philosophy does not believe in salvation: it places its trust solely in the free human act. However, the precondition for this is a personality that is capable of free human acts, that is to say, a personality which has given life meaning. Someone can only participate in rational value discussion and in the leading up to philosophical value discussion if they have given their life meaning. For this reason alone, it is radical philosophy's duty to be aware of the movements of radicalism of the feelings; to offer values and recommendations for forms of life by which it *is possible to live today* — to live according to the perspective of how one ought to live. Radical philosophy cannot shirk the task of giving an answer to the *existential problems* of human life.

We have just mentioned the existential problems of human

life, but here a qualification is necessary which today affects not just radical philosophy, but *every* philosophy. Philosophy wishes us to give a norm to the world or a world to the norm. Radical philosophy wishes the world to become a home for human beings. *The world as home for humanity* — that is the empire, the "garden" of philosophy, and its perspective concerns this empire. Everything that lies outside the world as home of humanity is not part of its empire, it is "jungle". The competence of philosophy includes existential questions which affect *human life* and which stem from the relationships of people to one another: it concerns the desire and the suffering which have their origin in people or in interpersonal relationships.

By contrast, *outside* the competence of philosophy lies that which creates in people a *feeling of giddiness*. Philosophy addresses the rational being and remains firmly within the sphere of what can be rationally thought: its rational utopia can always be thought rationally. What creates in the human imagination a feeling of giddiness cannot be thought of rationally; it cannot be the subject-matter of philosophy. People become giddy at the thought of the finitude or the infinitude of the universe: at the thought of death, at the thought of nothingness. In relation to what makes people giddy, *philosophy should be silent*. Philosophy has words for how one can *live with* the thought of death, but about nothingness it should be silent. Spinoza remarked that philosophy thinks of life, not of death, and so formulated very precisely the relationship of philosophy to this "feeling of giddiness": he excluded death as something for him that was non-existent. Philosophy cannot offer any substitute for the hereafter of religion.

Since radical philosophy has to give an answer to existential questions, it excludes those problems which make people "giddy", for no philosophy can give an answer to them. Equally little can they be answered by art, for art too always speaks only of life and deals with eternity, death, the finiteness of the world and of humanity as things which are part of human life. The empire of "giddiness" belongs only to religion, for this experience is of a religious nature. Anyone who does not want religion, anyone who rejects the religious experience, could not do better than to follow Spinoza's advice and exclude from their thought those things that make a person giddy.

(d) Radical philosophers have to be partial recipients of their own philosophy also in relation to the issue of "how should one act". Obviously the question of how one *should* act is inherent in their philosophical ideals. Yet they must also have proposals as to how one can act and what action is possible today, and obviously the answer stating what is possible must be sought and given on the basis of their own values. One duty of radical philosophy is therefore to make proposals for political action in the widest sense.

Radical philosophy does not believe in salvation, and it therefore cannot believe in any one single redeeming human act by which humanity is enabled to enter overnight the radical utopia as a land of milk and honey. It is a long and narrow path that leads to the radical utopia. Human beings are always confronted with concrete situations and conflicts, and in these concrete situations and concrete conflicts they must cope with the *possible*. Radical philosophy must never disdainfully look down from the heights of its utopia on people's attempts to solve their concrete conflicts and to act in a way that suits their concrete situation. It is its duty to think together with all those who attempt to solve concrete conflicts and who search for the possibilities of the best action in concrete situations. Its proposals for their actions have to be based on *two sorts of criteria*: the criterion of the ought of the rational utopia, and the criterion of the possible. It therefore has to criticise all proposals for action which run counter to the rational utopia and which lead in the opposite direction — this is the criterion of the ought. Simultaneously it has to take account of the room to manoeuvre for action and the empirical preconditions of action — the criterion of the possible. A radical philosophy which turns away from political activities which are in accordance with the possibilities turns away from its own realisation. It turns its utopia into a *nonrational* utopia.

By contrast, a radical philosophy which celebrates one step which is in accordance with the possibilities as "the" redeeming human act, abandons the radical *utopia* itself. If radical philosophy wants actually to remain radical philosophy, then it cannot give up either its utopia or its rationality.

Two further remarks are relevant with regard to the tasks of radical philosophy. The duties of radical philosophy have been briefly listed, obviously without assuming that *every single* radical philosopher could achieve them all. One cannot demand giftedness, for it is not a question of will but rather, as the word implies, a gift, and to achieve simultaneously all the tasks that have been enumerated would presuppose an exceptional giftedness. The demands were addressed to radical philosophy, and to achieve them could not be the work of a single person, but only of a multitude of persons. Yet there is one thing that one can demand of *every individual* radical philosopher, namely that they are partial recipients of at least *one* of the three areas of their rational utopia, that they apply their ought in at least *one sphere* of the possibilities, and that in at least *one way* they open the road that leads from the partial to the general, to the universal. Without this, they cannot be radical philosophers.

The second problem concerns the *negative possibilities* of the human future. Radical philosophy *cannot* build this possibility into its philosophical system. It formulates what *ought to be*: the positive possibilities of human development. Its vision is of the earth which will be the home of humanity, and of the humanity which will make the earth into its home. Radical philosophy cannot envisage nuclear self-destruction or ecological catastrophe, for the essence of radical utopia is precisely that it *excludes* these perspectives. However, as partial recipients of their own philosophy, radical philosophers take account of all possibilities, and therefore *cannot* exclude from their thought the fearful vision of the end of humanity. All their proposals, which involve how one here and now should think, live and act, must take account of this negative possibility, for it is one of their duties, and not the least of them, to work out *counter-alternatives* to the problems and conflicts which *can also* lead to the realisation of this negative possibility.

Radical philosophy therefore should apply the values of its rational utopia in the areas of critical social theory, philosophy of life and political theory, in order to be able to mobilise on its side every acting and thinking person and so contribute to ruling out humanity's negative alternatives. *Radical philosophy has to become praxis, so that praxis becomes theoretical*, so that people can raise themselves to the level of philosophical value discussion — before it is too late.

THE IDEALS OF LEFT-WING RADICALISM

What follows is an attempt to formulate the concrete and universal ideals of radical philosophy. The reference point for our ideals is humanity as the universal social group. In our ideals and in our interpretation of them we follow the criteria of the true value which we have already put forward. We therefore ascribe to our radical utopia guiding values, the universal validation of which itself guarantees and constitutes the *plurality of values* and the *plurality of forms of life*.

It is part of the idea of the radical utopia that it is committed to the abolition of the quasi-natural division of labour, to the abolition of conflicts of interest and hence to the abolition of interest regulation itself. If we posit a plurality of guiding values, this plurality does not express a multitude of conflicting interests, but is instead the pluralistic interpretation of the recommended value ideas. All interpretations of value ideas are different but equally true; the pluralism of value interpretations *expresses an affinity with the plurality of needs and of forms of life*. Today however, plurality of needs is expressed largely if not entirely in the plurality of interests and hence in conflicts of interest. We therefore have to conceive of a value with a claim to universal validity, and the universal observance of this value must presuppose that needs are *not* expressed through the mediation of interests. It must be assumed that if our guiding values are to be universal, then each of the many needs must be purged of every element of interest — the need satisfaction of certain groups of people will not in principle collide with the need satisfaction of another group. This is the only way in which *the progress of humanity* can be conceived. If we are however to conceive continual progress in *this* direction, then we must assume that the leading values which we will later put forward are already accepted as value ideas, and that they are therefore thought to be universally valid. We therefore must posit an *initial consensus* which accepts these values as *regulative theoretical and practical ideas*, and hence we must posit a consensus as to the validity of value ideas of the radical utopia. We cannot conceptualise this consensus as the outcome of "continual progress". We have to presuppose a *virtual starting point* concerning the *validity of the value ideas*, so that we can begin to conceive the continual progress towards their universal observance.

As we know, within the value ideals of philosophy the *ultimate* ideal is always the *most general-universal* or the *most singular-individual*. The substance is either God, nature or monads; the species being is either humankind or the personality. Whatever a philosophy posits as a mere particular value cannot ever also be its ultimate value.

In the rational-immanent utopia of radical philosophy *the two ultimate values* — as the most general-universal and the most singular-individual — coincide. Marx's own philosophical vision — at least as far as it can be found in the *Economic and Philosophical Manuscripts* — was undoubtedly that through the abolition of alienation every individual would become identical with the human species. For us this complete identification is *inconceivable*. We therefore interpret Marx's vision in the following way. Alienation will be abolished and it will be possible to speak of a "societised humankind" when every individual person has *a conscious relation to the human species*. "Identity" means to say that every individual can appropriate the totality of the wealth of the human species; "conscious relation" means to say that every individual can choose from the wealth of humanity what they need for the multi-faceted and rich development of their own personality. The development of the wealth of the human species and the development of the wealth of the personality are therefore processes that mutually involve each other. To this extent the two ultimates — the most general-universal and the most singular-individual — do in fact coincide in the community of free people.

The values which guide the construction of our rational-immanent utopia, and hence the values which we must want to raise into value ideas, therefore have to be values which express the coincidence of these two "ultimates". For the ideals of radical philosophy we must choose those values which are *true values*, which therefore can be related without contradiction to the value ideas that today are universally valid — above all with the highest good, freedom. These values also have to be values which can be conceived together with *all* values which reveal an affinity with radical needs, it must be possible to apply them to the same value ideals, and it must be possible for them to *be validated together*.

At the same time we have to put forward value ideas which *can be interpreted in different ways*. Obviously we cannot say anything about these interpretations themselves, we can only formulate the relevant ought — that they *ought to be different*, for we do after all presuppose a plurality of needs and of forms of life. If we were to say anything about the interpretations of the value ideals of the future, then that would be a utopian utopia. However, constructing utopian utopias is the concern of poetry — Fourier was also a poet — and not of philosophy.

However I am positing guiding values which enable, and in a certain sense even demand, a conscious relationship to value ideas and to the wish that all interpretations of values be true. I therefore can assume the will of true human beings to raise certain true values to value ideas and their will to relate all their values to these value ideas. I can therefore posit *the moral personality*.

The higher a value stands, the more the relationship to it presupposes a moral content. As the starting point of value rational action, every idea of value also implies a moral attitude. From this it follows that the ideas of value in which the two ultimates — the ultimate universal and the ultimate individual — coincide, also posit a *new moral world order*.

We ascribe three ideals to the radical utopia:

(a)   The first ideal is *identical* with the one that has been formulated and partly analysed by Apel and Habermas. This is the ideal of "domination-free communication" which presupposes an "ideal communication society". As Habermas describes the radical utopia, in it "the basic norms of reasonable speech can be elevated to the organisational principle of a process of opinion creation which is discursively justified, in other words which interprets needs in a way which allows them to be revised."

In fact in both formulations this value is an "ultimate" ideal, for in it the most universal and the most singular coincide. "Reasonable speech" is posited partly as the organising principle, that is to say, as the general and universal institution for the solution of the problems of societised humanity. At the same time it also appears as a value for the personality, since in a society which posits symmetrical relationships, everybody — as individual entities, as equally reasonable beings and as individuals — participates in the "process of will formation" which this institution guarantees.

The "ideal communication society" is nothing other than the realisation of the idea of democracy. Up to now it has not been possible for the ideal of democracy to be achieved in its totality in any historical or contemporary democratic society: at most one or other aspect of it, one particular concrete meaning of it or one value interpretation of it has been realised. In fact, every society based on relationships of subordination and superordination presupposes domination, in other words, an unequal distribution of power and an unequal control over goods and people in the society. This occurs either by certain classes, strata or castes possessing power and excluding from it all other classes, strata or castes, or by certain classes, strata or castes at least possessing more power than others, since through use of their institutions they are more able than others to control the goods and people of the society. The total realisation of democracy is identical with the abolition of all domination. It therefore involves an equal distribution of power, for that presupposes that *every person* disposes over the material goods and people of the society; it presupposes that there is no sphere over which or in which people cannot control. In a society free of domination *all people* decide — as reasonable beings — questions of administrative power in the course of distinct and concrete value discussions.

"Every person has *equal* power" could also mean that *nobody* possesses any power. I personally do not consider that this "reversal" can be rationally achieved. I would like once again to point out what was said about the possibility of isolating personal relationships of dependency from relationships of subordination and superordination. Every person should participate in value discussion as an equally reasonable being: every person should participate equally in the determination of values, in the working out of the society's strategy of action — the action of all the communities of the society. This is what we mean when we speak of equal power for everyone. By claiming that nobody should possess any power we would also exclude from the rational utopia personal relationships of dependency. This would rule out any possibility that greater specialist knowledge enjoyed relative authority in questions of purposive rational action. It would make it impossible for society to entrust those who had a greater specialist knowledge and authority with the carrying out of purposive rational action. Without this relative authority (and the power that it involves) any society of any complexity at all would be paralysed. The model of a realisable radical democracy therefore does not exclude *conflicts*. The generalisation, to say nothing of the permanence and institutionalisation, of philosophical value discussion precisely has to prevent relationships of personal dependency reproducing a society based on relationships of subordination and superordination.

Radical democracy must take on an institutionalised form. Naturally that does not mean that every discussion of true values has to occur within institutions. People have to decide on their own responsibility for which value discussions the institutions are responsible and for which ones they are not. The achievement of democracy is only conceivable together with *the democratic personality*. The two fundamental aspects which Habermas characterises as "the universalisation of the basic norms and the internalisation of the controls over behaviour" are two interwoven aspects of one and the same process.

The domination-free value discussion associated with the ideal communication society is conceived as a discussion of true values. In the sense of our ideals, every person has *the right and the duty* to join in the controversy over true values, there to bring to bear rational arguments, to determine and to interpret values.

Habermas ascribes three fundamental values to the ideal communication society as value ideas: truth, justice and freedom. We do not dispute that this ascription is justified: we accept his value idea as true, we recognise that the three concrete values which he lists can be ascribed to it without contradiction. However, our question is whether this value idea exhausts all value ideas corresponding to the radical utopia. Our question is whether other values related to freedom as the highest good and the universally valid value idea cannot *equally* be raised to the level of ideals.

These questions are completely justified. The ideal concretised above concerns only *one* of the features which characterise the human species: namely that human beings are reasonable and rational beings capable of argument. Yet the human beings on which this ideal is based are not *complete* human beings. They have *no bodies*, *no feelings* and equally they have *no interpersonal relationships*. Their relationship to each other is constituted exclusively by value discussion. They do not need to be human beings at all — they could just as well be angels. However, we do not want to design our radical utopia for angels. Human beings are certainly rational beings, but they are not *only* that.

What sort of ideal corresponds to the "domination-free communication society"? What sort of ideal does it posit and what sort of an ideal does it express? *It is the ideal of "the true" from the standpoint of the radical utopia* and the concrete generalisation of the value judgement "Not this is true, but that is true" from the standpoint of radical philosophy. It contains the general idea of the "true": from the standpoint of our ideals, what is true is what reasonably thinking and arguing people agree to be true. It contains the idea of "the true value", for it is based on the ideal of philosophical value discussion. This "true" is — like the idea of "true" in every philosophy — "the true as good". At the same time as the true is constituted, so also is a system of rights and duties, for in the discussion of true values *justice* asserts itself. The constitution of the true belongs to the *freedom* of every individual person. *The true as good is however not the good itself: the true is merely one aspect of the highest good.*

(b) Apel formulates the *morality* of the future communication society as follows: "Whenever a person argues, then that person implicitly recognises all possible claims of all members of the communication society which can be justified by reasonable argument . . . Human needs are ethically relevant as interpersonally communicable 'claims'; they must be recognised in so far as they can be interpersonally justified through arguments."

However, if someone says to me, "I need you", can I then answer them with: "I am prepared to recognise your need to the extent that you first justify your claim with reasonable arguments"? This is certainly something I cannot do. Only two answers are possible: either "Here I am", or "I am not able to satisfy your need." However, there is one thing I certainly can *not* do, and that is to expect, still less demand, that this need is supported or confirmed by arguments.

If someone says to me, "I need that", can I then answer them by saying that I will only recognise their need when they justify it with reasonable arguments? I certainly cannot do this. I can either say to them, "Here, take it", or "I am not in a position to give you what you need, for this or that reason." However, there is one thing I certainly can *not* do, and that is to expect, still less demand, that they justify their need with reasonable arguments. *It is not the person who turns to me with their need who has to argue; rather, in so far as I cannot satisfy their need, it is I who have to argue.*

This is not to say that one cannot justify needs. However, it is clear that in the overwhelming majority of cases the justification of needs *occurs by reference to other needs*. Either one cannot rationally justify needs at all, or one justifies them by other needs. In the justification of needs it is only in very exceptional cases that one can step *outside* needs themselves. The totality of needs cannot be brought into the discussion, for the discussion has its *limits*. If a producing community explains that it needs particular machines, then one can demand that this is justified with arguments. The answer will probably run: "Because with them work would be easier and free time longer" — but this is in turn an enumeration of needs. One could go a step further and say, "Argue why your work should be easier and why you need more free time", and the answer would probably run, "Because we would like not to be so terribly exhausted, and we would like to concern ourselves with things which we would like to do but for which we don't have the time" — *once again* therefore an enumeration of needs.

The recognition of the needs of others therefore cannot depend upon whether or not they are rationally explained. *The needs of others have to be recognised unconditionally.* To the extent that we are not in the position to satisfy them, then it is *we* who have to justify that. If we cannot satisfy a need, *we cannot question the need itself.*

A world in which one had to justify every need would stand *morally even lower* than the one in which we live. The ideal of the communication society therefore cannot be related to the good as the moral ideal of the future. We do not want a morality which *exhausts itself in a system of rights and duties*. We do not want to posit as an ideal a morality which excludes or neglects all moral values *apart from duty*. We do not want to posit as an ideal a morality which shuts its eyes to the values of immediate human relationships: to friendship, goodness, love and love of one's nearest; to sympathy, thankfulness and generosity. We do not want to posit as an ideal a morality which does not take into account that the other — the other person and their needs — is for me an unconditional value which lies beyond all doubt. For if someone whom we love says, "I need you", then we can only say, "Here I am." If the need — the person of the other — is a value which I cannot question, then to the person who says, "I need that", I can only say, "It does not concern me *why* you need that — take it." The relationship of rational argument is *not* a relationship of love.

Let us take one more look at what has been said of morality. The good is a value orientation category which has imperative character; morality is — at least in the first instance — a system of rules, the essence of which is that it *ought* to be preferred above all other social rule systems. However, the rules of this system of rules are always concretely formulated in a network of interrelated norms; it is always the *duty* of people to act according to these norms. An interrelated network of norms, so it was said, but this interrelationship is not always coherent. The system of moral rules frequently involves numerous different and even mutually contradictory norms of behaviour, and it demands that every individual person applies these rules. The norms differ according to class, stratum and even objectification: someone who from one point of view is fulfilling their duty may not be fulfilling it from another. As a result of the *alienation of morality* it becomes ever more difficult for the individual consciously to reflect upon the dilemma of morality, consciously to take it upon themselves and to bring it to fruition. Every individual is entangled in a network of heterogeneous duties which are *not* appropriate to them as individuals. Hence they are compelled to question the validity of the norms, or not to allow them any effectiveness or simply to subsume their deeds under one valid value, in that they neglect the concrete situation, their own personality and the person whom the need affects. Alienated morality admittedly develops certain abilities, but at the same time it allows others to decay. *The person who stumbles around in the jungle of duties can never become a moral personality.*

Kant wanted to solve this dilemma by excluding every concrete duty and instead setting up the general formula of following the duty. However, with this he merely expressed in the form of a new theory that morality is a system of rules which should be preferred to all other systems of rules. This reproduces the same problems — if not in the theory, then nonetheless for anyone who has made the Kantian categorical imperative their own — which Kant attempted to minimise. If duty has no content, then "the" duty does not exist either. Once again however, this same ethic eliminates the dilemma of morality, in that it excludes action from ethics.

The Critique of Practical Reason is suited to the bourgeois world epoch: it is doubtless its most systematic ethics. That is, it posits the empirical person of bourgeois society — the person described in Hobbes' anthropology — who is ab ovo *unsuited* to reflect and take upon themselves the dilemma of morality.

If the community of rationally arguing people is posited as the single, ultimate ideal of value, and if one ascribes a morality to this community, then all that has happened is that Kant's ethics have been given a social form. Here too only one single duty matters: the duty of rational argument. As we have seen with Apel, this constitutes morality. For Kant however, only the moral personality is a purely rational being, but not however the human person itself. Kant also recognises the homo phenomenon, and homo noumenon gives the law to homo phenomenon. However, the community of rationally arguing people is also a *community of people who act*, it is also a community of empirical human beings. In such a community of people who act, one cannot and must not conceive of the person purely as a rational being. The rational utopia addresses a personality who as an empirical person, and not merely as a rational being, is also a moral being: a person who has both the possibility and the ability consciously to think through and apply the dilemma of morality, a person who on their own responsibility — going beyond duty — is able to act, a person who also satisfies a need even when it is not justified by arguments, a person who is — the simple, hackneyed word is apposite — a *good person*.

Lukács made two proposals for overcoming the ethics of duty. In his early works he divided ethics into the so-called "first" and "second" ethics. The "second ethics" is the *ethics of the good*, beyond duty. In the bourgeois world, the period of "completed sinfulness", this ethics reaches only a few: the good is "mercy". The "ethics of the good" can only be generalised in communities. In his late works Lukács completely and utterly rejects the ethics of duty, to replace it with *the ethics of the personality*.

For our part we would like to make the following comments on this. We cannot conceive of any ethics from which duty can be eliminated. To repeat once again: the good is an imperative value orientation category and as such has a constitutive social function. Morality is, in the first instance, a system of rules which has to be given priority over all other systems of rules. There is no system of rules without rules; there is no morality without norms which have to be given priority over all other rules — norms are rules which every person ought to obey and which therefore impose duties upon us. At the same time however, for the radical utopia we posit a morality which goes beyond duty: *an ethics of the personality and of the good*, an ethic which does *not* divide people into homo phenomenon and homo noumenon.

We conceive the resolution of this issue as follows. We seek value ideas for the radical utopia which — as value ideas — are *unconditionally normative*, which it is the duty of every person to recognise as valid and to *want* to achieve. Simultaneously, these norms have to be of a nature such that their observance ought not only to include what lies beyond duty, but also precisely *to presuppose it. They have to be of a type such that their observance does not involve the following of any concrete rules.* We are therefore looking for universally valid values, the observance of which *in every case* presupposes the conscious recognition of the dilemma of morality and the acceptance of responsibility for this dilemma — their observance has to presuppose both personal responsibility and the personality that takes on this responsibility. They are therefore guiding values, *the universal validity of which is expressed and constituted in actual actions that themselves make no claim for universal validity.*

So far we have seen that if one only posits domination-free

communication, one does not get beyond an ethics of duty. In order to think our utopia through to the end, we therefore *also* have to posit additional guiding values.

One way Kant's genius showed itself was that he knew that which his successors forgot: namely that his ethics has to be supplemented by values of this sort. Therefore in the *Metaphysics of Morals* he included in his system two material values: firstly *the perfection of oneself*, secondly *the happiness of the other*.

Perfection of oneself implies that it is the duty of every person to perfect their own ability according to their personality, their gifts and their situation. This is also a value with a claim to universal validity. However, since every person has a different personality, different abilities and different gifts, and finds themselves in different situations, it can *only* be achieved in actions without any claim to universal validity.

According to Kant, the happiness of the other above all implies that we discover what makes the other person happy. In this way this value cannot and does not produce any universal norm. Every other person, and *only* they, knows what happiness involves for them. If one desires the happiness of all people and if it is our duty to desire it, then in every individual case one has to proceed *differently*. This universally valid value can therefore also *only* be achieved in actions without any claim to universal validity.

If we put together the two ideas of material duty formulated by Kant with Marx's ideal of humanity, then we reach *two* ultimate values which should be posited as the value ideas of the radical utopia. If this happens, then we reach an ethics, which *certainly refers to duty, but which goes beyond duty*.

First we want to interpret the material duty "happiness of the other" from the point of view of the Marxian ideal of humanity. This value, which we are recommending should be accepted as a value idea and which we therefore formulate with a claim to universal validity, consists in the *recognition and acceptance of all other human needs*. This value idea is "the ideal of the good" in our rational utopia. Yet every value which we propose should be generalised as a value idea must be able to be related without contradiction to the value ideas valid *today*, in particular to the highest good, to freedom. Without this, our value cannot be a true value. One interpretation, one meaning of freedom as an value idea, which we can relate without contradiction to this ideal and which cannot be contradicted by any other interpretation, is expressed in the following norm of Kant's: "No human being should serve as a mere means for another human!"

Our value must *not contradict* this norm. If it did contradict it, then it would not be a true value and we could not make any claim for its universal validity. We can therefore only formulate the ideal of "the good" in the following way: "*The recognition and acceptance of all human needs, in so far as this excludes the use of other people as a mere means.*" This value corresponds to all the criteria which we have presupposed in relation to the ideals of value of the radical utopia. Since the need of every person should be recognised, this value refers to the ultimate universal, to *humankind*. Since the need of every person as an individual is to be recognised, this value relates to the ultimate individual entity, to the *personality*. At the same time it is a value which not only ensures *the plurality of needs*, but precisely *presupposes* it. As we have seen, it is a norm which can only be universally observed if its application in concrete action makes no claim to universal validity. It requires the recognition and satisfaction of the *distinctive* — and always concrete — need of every individual person. This is the only way I can understand the Marxist formula "To each according to their need".

Kant was right: love is *not* a duty. When however I say, "Recognise the need of every person and satisfy it", then the value of love is based on this norm, just as all values of interpersonal human relations are also based in it: friendship, generosity, understanding, tact, sympathy and, above all, goodness. If someone whom we love says, "I need you", then one can only answer, "Here I am."

However, philosophy at the same time also has to constitute "the good" as *true*. The ideals of the true, the good and the beautiful must not contradict each other: each contains the other, and they all are related to the highest good. We have presented "domination-free communication", the institutionalised philosophical value discussion, as the guiding ideal of our radical utopia: it is the ideal of the *true*. We assume that realised democracy and the democratic personality that corresponds to it constitute *true value*. We have to link the ideal of the good to this ideal, *so that the good can be true*.

The values which express an affinity to needs have to be the subject of rational and philosophical value discussion. *The need itself* however cannot be the subject of value discussion. The need — so states the ideal of the good — has to be unconditionally recognised. Hence the value discussion cannot revolve around the question of whether or not we can recognise the other's need. If someone says to us "I need you" or "I need that", then two sorts of answer are possible. Either "Here I am" (or "Here, take it"), or "I cannot satisfy your need". As we have seen, this last answer requires arguments to justify it.

In order to avoid misunderstandings, let us once again stress what the unconditional recognition of need means. Every need must be recognised which does not contradict a fundamental interpretation of the ideal of freedom and the norm which follows from it, namely that human beings should not serve as a mere means for other humans. It is therefore self-evidently a relevant question for philosophical value discussion, whether or not the satisfaction of an emergent need demanding satisfaction involves regarding other people as a mere means.

The *ideal of the good* contains two aspects: the recognition of all needs, *and* the satisfaction of all needs. "Every need must be recognised" is a *constitutive idea*; "Every need must be satisfied" is a *regulative idea*. We act under the guidance of regulative ideas and we accept the idea as universally valid; it is however part of the essence of regulative ideas that their observance is only conceivable as an *infinite process*.

For the philosophical value discussion which the radical utopia presupposes it is not a question *whether* all needs can be satisfied. Just like the philosophical value discussion, this discussion posits as true values all values, and all of them show an affinity to needs. Philosophical value discussion concerns which true value should be given *priority* in relation to concrete decisions, in relation to decisions concerning action, in relation to the strategy of action. In other words, practical value discussion places in a hierarchy the needs to which the values manifest an affinity.

If the value discussion revolves around whether or not a need is a "real" need, and if the recognition of a need is made to depend on the need being supported by rational arguments, then the discussion is *not democratic*. How could anyone claim for themselves the right to question whether or not a need is "real"? The subject-matter of the democratic value discussion is not whether or not the need of the other should be recognised, and equally, its subject-matter is not whether the claim of the need to be satisfied should be recognised or not. Democratic value discussion concerns the following: "If I satisfy your need, then I cannot satisfy someone else's, and if I satisfy their need, then I cannot satisfy yours. Come, we want to think together, we want to seek the truth together! Which need — and which value with an affinity to this need — should we prefer? I know that both needs ought to be satisfied, for that is a regulative idea. But here and now both needs cannot be satisfied. We therefore should together decide which need we ought to choose, and which need it is more important that we satisfy!"

Every person participates as a *rational being* in the democratic philosophical value discussion. In this discussion people do not have to declare their needs, but rather the values which express an affinity to their needs. In the course of the argument — but only then — the participant has to abstract their values from their needs in the way that the formula for responsibility in philosophical value discussion lays down. More precisely, they have to abstract their values from everything that is *particularistic* in their needs. That is their duty. At the same time in every value discussion they have the *right* also to abstract from how a value is connected to the need of *another person*, or more precisely, to abstract from everything that is *particularistic* in the need of the other.

At the same time however, people are *not only rational beings*. From the perspective of philosophical value discussion they certainly are rational beings, but they also participate in it as *indivisible personalities*. As indivisible personalities it is *not their duty to insist on their right*. Since the satisfaction of the needs of others is a value idea of the radical utopia, and since this ideal imposes on everyone a regulative idea, we can presuppose people who *will understand the regulative idea as constitutive* in relation to others. One can therefore presuppose people who give priority to a value *because* it shows an affinity to the needs of *others* and not to their own. This attitude is not a precondition for the philosophical value discussion, and it is *not* a part of the democratic personality; it characterises *the good person*.

Doubtless however, in mediated human relationships the good — and love — is not the *usual* basic attitude. The institutionalised forms of philosophical value discussion are certainly suited to such mediated human relationships. It is in fact not possible to conceive of any society in which the majority of interpersonal relationships were not *mediated*.

People are involved in unmediated human contacts through their concrete personalities: they are not involved as purely rational beings, but rather always and necessarily as *whole personalities*. Hence in such situations people cannot abstract from either their own or others' individuality. This individuality is always *unique*, and even in its conscious relationship to the human species it involves the uniqueness of the individual's qualities and of the individual's point of view. In such relationships, mutually related needs are always of a *qualitative* sort. The highest value which shows an affinity to these needs is always the other person, *the uniqueness of the other person*. There are no philosophical value discussions in relation to unmediated human relationships, or more precisely, to the extent that there are any, partly they are uninstitutionalised and partly they concern not the values of the relationship itself, but other values. Hence, here there are no rights and no duties: friendship and love are not rights and they are not duties. In direct human relationships the recognition *and* the satisfaction of the need of the other are equally constitutive ideas. The moment this ceases, then the relationship itself is dissolved, but even when this occurs a philosophical argument is neither necessary nor possible. The collapse of a relationship means that we confront a need with the lack of need. To "I need you!" we respond: "I cannot satisfy your need, for on my side there is no longer any need." Any other argument is false, for it would be nothing more than mere rationalisation.

The number of unmediated human relationships is small, but these relationships are precisely what is *fundamental* in human lives. We therefore conceive the radical utopia as a society in which the ideal of the good is achieved in its two aspects as a constitutive idea in people's most fundamental relationships. These are the relationships — including the relationships of friendship within freely chosen communities — in which the achievement of the value of the good becomes people's second nature. The personality which is here constituted by the ideal of the good is more than a democratic personality: it is already a *moral personality*.

(c) As the starting point of the *third ideal* of our radical utopia, we choose the duty to perfect oneself. This is the value which has the highest place in Marx's value hierarchy: the wealth of humankind. We know that in Marx's theory the precondition for the abolition of alienation is the identity of the human species and the individual; that therefore the "wealth of humankind" means the wealth of the human species and at the same time the wealth of the personality and the individual. "The wealth of the human species" means *the development of all the material, psychic and spiritual abilities that characterise the species*. "The wealth of the personality" means *the appropriation and development of all these material, psychic and spiritual abilities by every individual in the society*.

Since we do not presuppose any complete identity between the species and the individual, but do presuppose a conscious relationship of all human beings to the human species and to themselves as members of the species, we would formulate this ideal as follows: "The development of all material, psychic and spiritual abilities of the human species, and the many-sided and harmonious development of individuals' *own* material, psychic and spiritual abilities by the appropriation of the wealth of the species in a way that is *suited to their own personality*". This formulation posits that *each* person can appropriate the given level of the wealth of society, so that the value treats humanity as the most general fundamental value. It also presupposes that each person achieves wealth through development of their *own* abilities and needs: the value therefore treats the personality as the most unique fundamental value.

The development of people's entire material, psychic and spiritual abilities means amongst other things: the development of the ability and the need to act; the development of the ability and the need to feel and to enjoy; the development of the ability and the need for taste; the development of the ability and the need for theoretical attitude; the development of the ability and the need for personal contact. It also presupposes a *harmony* amongst all these abilities and needs. The many-sided and harmonious person with developed needs and abilities is the *beautiful person*. Our third ideal is therefore the ideal of the *beautiful*. If the earth is to be the home of humanity, then beauty ought also to "be at home". Beauty can find its home in the ability of all to create and enjoy beauty — from everyday life up to the highest objects of art.

The philosophical ideal of the beautiful cannot however make itself independent of the ideal of the good, just as little as it can make itself independent of the ideal of the true. Above all, this ideal cannot contradict the highest good, namely freedom. It *ought* to be conceivable together with all values that involve freedom. That is to say, all values that concern the development of human needs and abilities must also *exclude from their ranks all those needs which relate to the other person as a mere means*.

It is people's *quantitative* needs that presuppose the degradation of other people to mere means — greed, ambition, lust for power. The purely quantitative needs therefore have to be excluded from the world of needs of the beautiful. However, this exclusion in no way contradicts the ideal of the beautiful, on the contrary, it is the *condition* for its achievement. For the development of the purely quantitative needs corrodes the personality; such needs are not preconditions, but rather the greatest obstacles to the development of a many-sided person rich in material, pyschic and spiritual needs. If the needs are multi-faceted, then the *quantification* of a qualitative need *puts limits on another qualitative need*.

The ideal of the beautiful is linked to the ideal of the good in another way. The development of the abilities of both humanity and the personality also imposes *duties* on the personality. That means to say that the ideal of the beautiful also contains *a normative* aspect. It is a valid value which *can only be observed individually* and the achievement of which cannot therefore make any claim to universal validity. After all, each person has to develop their *own* abilities and needs on the basis of a conscious relationship to the human species and to their own human nature, but each person is unique and unrepeatable. This is the only way I can interpret Marx's "From each according to their abilities". This is therefore an ideal which not only allows *plurality*, but also presupposes it: a plurality of needs, of abilities, of forms of life.

Let us now turn to the relationship between the ideal of the beautiful and the ideal of the true. Just like the ideal of the good, the ideal of the beautiful also contains two aspects: on the one hand, the development of the wealth of society, on the other hand, the appropriation of this wealth in a manner appropriate to the personality through the multi-faceted development of the abilities and needs of every individual human being.

The development of the wealth of society can for its part only be a *regulative* idea. Namely, this idea presupposes an *infinite process* in the development of knowledge and culture, social production included. In brief, it presupposes that society is *dynamic*: one can never claim that the wealth of society exists *already*.

The *how* of the social dynamic — what objectifications should be concretely developed and in what tempo this should be done — can only be *decided* in a democratic value discussion, in which each person participates as a *rational being* and as a member of the community of the participants in the discussion. Every participant must be guided by the regulative idea that the wealth of the society *ought* to be developed. By contrast, which concrete value should have priority is something that has to be continually decided anew in a rational discussion which weighs up all the true values.

The democratic value discussion has *no* competence to decide which abilities or which needs a personality or a community ought to develop at a *given* level of social wealth, just as it has no competence to decide how the harmony or the form of life of the personality should be arranged. The explanation "These are my abilities, these are what I want to develop" is just as final as is the claim "This is my need." It too is beyond argument.

Let us pause here a moment. The shaping of our abilities and the shaping of our needs is *one and the same process*. If we claim that the other person's need ought to be recognised unconditionally, then we are also claiming that their competence to develop their abiltities has to be unconditionally recognised too. Here again no argument is required. It is impossible to imagine any form of democratic value discussion which could be competent in this area. However, does this mean that all forms of a *critique of needs* have to be excluded from our rational utopia?

I cannot imagine any society which *suited human beings* in which there could be no critique of needs at all. However, the democratic value discussion is not the locus of the critique of needs. Instead, if the critique of needs is not to become a tyranny of needs, one can only imagine it occurring within immediate and personal human relationships. The critique must not question the needs of the other person, for the other person's needs have to be recognised unconditionally, just as values which express an affinity to the other person's needs have to be recognised as true values. Needs are the basis of the sphere of immediate personal relationships. Hence the critique of needs can only be posed as *advice*. The precondition for this advice is that the other person — *this* concrete person — counts for me as a value. For this reason alone, the critique of needs cannot be the subject-matter of a democratic value discussion.

When critique takes the form of advice, then the leading value which guides it is that of the third ideal (i.e. the beautiful), considered from the point of view of the observance of the second ideal (i.e. the good). One person says to another person (and does so because they are important to them, because they love them): "I recognise your need, but I consider, I think, I feel, that you could develop more of your abilities; you have abilities which these needs do not further, but rather contradict." However, *verbalisation* is at most one aspect of this critique — the essence of it is *helping*. The critique of needs is *advice*, because in it the determining factor is not rational argument but rather *active love*. The active love of the critique of needs is a *means of education*. Yet the institutionalised philosophical value discussion is not an educational institution, and equally, value discussion itself — in its non-institutionalised form — is not a mutual education, but at most an aspect of it. I therefore term the critique of needs advice, for this critique always starts with the recognition of the other person's need and is always a mutual process.

To develop one's own abilities and the corresponding needs, to appropriate as necessary the given wealth of the society — this is conceived as a *constitutive idea* of our radical utopia, and can also be thought of as such. People are of course finite beings; the development of their abilities and of the corresponding needs therefore cannot be unlimited. It is not the job of society to ensure that individuals "economise" with their abilities and needs: the finiteness of life takes care of that. Human beings do have to master their abilities and needs, for the development of *all* qualitative needs contradicts our human condition.

Up to now we have been discussing how individuals may develop their own abilities by appropriating the wealth of society at its given level. Up to now we have been discussing two ultimates, humanity and the personality. However, humanity cannot be the *only* reference point for the development of human abilities. The elaboration of abilities presupposes a *task*, and furthermore, it presupposes the others who set the task or whom the task concerns. The need for recognition is an inherent human need. Human beings develop their abilities for the sake of others and not only for themselves, they want their personality to be recognised, they see the confirmation of their achievements in recognition *by others*.

Radical democracy, as the institutionalised system of the philosophical value discussion, regulates mediated human relationships. Individuals participate in this discussion as purely rational beings. However, human beings are not just rational beings. They do not just want the truth of their values to be recognised, they cannot just be satisfied merely by participation in rational discussion. Democratic value discussion develops one single ability and one single need: the ability and the need for rational argument. Yet — in the sense of the ideal of the beautiful — a constitutive idea of the rational utopia is that human beings should harmoniously develop numerous qualitatively different abilities and needs. Human abilities cannot develop without community. Only a *community* can *pose personal tasks*; only a community can ensure the recognition of endeavour and the recognition of all development of abilities and of all endeavours, *independent* of the overall social relevance, the novelty and the weight of the achievement.

For this reason we can only conceive our radical utopia as a society of individuals who are freely united in communities. The development of new forms of life is tantamount to the development of new human relationships. There is no private form of life. The achievement of the ideal of the beautiful therefore also presupposes *the development of free and beautiful forms of human intercourse*. Forms of social life are free and beautiful when the community furthers rather than hinders the multi-faceted development of human abilities and needs. The structure of people's abilities and needs varies. We therefore imagine the radical utopia as having communities with differing forms of life. In other words, we posit *the plurality of forms of life*.

If therefore we want to link what ought to be to what is, if we are interpreting what has to be done immediately from the point of view of what ought to be, then we cannot see in the plurality of forms of life that exist today any obstacle that has to be overcome. The radical utopia can be developed from the existing plurality of forms of life, in that the form of life is no longer determined by interest, but rather by need, and by free autonomous choice instead of by convention.

AUTONOMY AND PLURALITY OF FORMS OF LIFE

Each of the three concretised ideals involves the dominance of different relationships. Thus, from the standpoint of the ideal of the "true" the dominant relationship is that of *the person to society* (i.e. the human being as *rational* being); from the standpoint of the "good" it is that of *the person to other human beings* (the human being as *empathising being*); from the standpoint of the ideal of the "beautiful" it is that of *the person to the community* (the human being as *creative* and *enjoying* being). However, persons are wholes: the democratic person, the moral person and the creative person are one and the same person. The person as democratic, moral and creative being, the person who achieves all these ideals together, such a person is the *autonomous* and *free* individual.

All three ideals which have been described here depend on *freedom*. Freedom is the *highest good*, and the three ideals are merely its forms of appearance. If these values became universally valid, then, and then alone, this would mean that the value idea of "freedom" would be binding as a universal norm. Philosophy is no god: it can certainly say, "Let there be light," but this would not remove the darkness.

If we formulated these ideas with a claim for universal validity, we would be saying: we *will* values to show an affinity with needs and not with interests; we will the end of society based on relationships of surbordination and superordination, on the inherited division of labour and on domination; we will the hypothetical starting point on which there is a *consensus* in relation to these ideas as ideas. Further, we *will* a consensus to be achieved in relation to *these* ideas, for we will human beings to agree on value ideas which guarantee *plurality*: the plurality of personalities, the plurality of forms of life. *In other words, we will a consensus which excludes any consensus in relation to all concrete values and all concrete theories.* For what we do *not* will is that there be only one true interpretation of *Hamlet* and what we do *not* will to conceive is that — in whatever context — only one good, one true and correct action or one recommendation for action should be possible.

Yet how can we conceive of this, when we have also posited the person as an *autonomous* being?

The philosophical value discussion is a discussion between true values. It can be a theoretical or a practical discussion. In theoretical discussion we are not under any pressure to act, so it is easy to conceive of this discussion as a discussion between autonomous persons, even when there is no consensus in relation to the values or the theories. Every discussion partner recognises that the other person's value is true and that their own true value reveals an affinity to their own needs. Therefore they apply this value autonomously in their theory, just as the other person can autonomously apply values with an affinity to their own needs in their own theory. There will be many values with an affinity to the systems of needs, and there will be many interpretations of *Hamlet*, but none of these interpretations will rob the creator and subject of the other interpretations of their autonomy. Hence the discussion can remain a genuine discussion. It can revolve around *which* theory is more complete and more beautiful, or it can involve the mutual relationship between understanding and misunderstanding. Essentially, the discussion addresses the "third person" — the person who is to accept the interpretation of one or other discussion partner. And it is no bad thing if one group accepts this interpretation and another that interpretation; rather this is precisely what is desirable. After all, a consensus over concrete values would exclude what should not be excluded: the creation and development of values and the precondition for this, the dynamic of society. A consensus on the true is only fruitful in the *pragmatic* side of the natural sciences.

Practical discussion however is dominated by the pressure for action. Within a given period of time one has to decide which action, recommended by which true value, is to be preferred, and that here and now. In this case the problem is not so simple. For, if the first ideal — the ideal of philosophical value discussion — were the sole ideal of the radical utopia, *then we ought to want a consensus to be created in all practical value discussions*, since if this did not occur, then there would always be people whose action was *not autonomous* and who would therefore come into contradiction with the highest good, with freedom.

If however the guiding ideals include accepting and satisfying the needs of others, then this makes it conceivable for an *autonomous action* to occur also *without* any consensus having arisen in value discussions. In this case each person can say: "Certainly you have not convinced me that this value is preferable for the action, but you have convinced me that this value shows an affinity to your needs. I accept this need and *want to satisfy it* — we will therefore act according to your value." A consensus concerning the true is only fruitful in legislation.

It is also conceivable that *autonomous* action can occur *without* any consensus having arisen in value discussions if the guiding values also include the multi-faceted development of abilities. For in this case it is possible to say: "Certainly, you have not convinced me that this value should be chosen to guide our action. Yet you have convinced me that acting according to the value which you are putting forward offers a new *task*; you have convinced me that it is a challenge which, if I rise to it, will enable me to test and develop my abilities. I can therefore improve myself in ways in which for a long time I could not: let us therefore act according to your value."

To the extent that we believe in the unity of humanity, we ought unconditionally to presuppose a system of representation which enables communities to be *represented* in any philosophical discussion of values which express an affinity to the common needs of these communities. If this occurs, then in all practical value discussions the representative of the community can fall back on the second and the third ideal of value — the ideal of the good and the ideal of the beautiful.

Within symmetrical relationships there are not only equal opportunities to participate in the value discussion, but also equal opportunities to *interrupt* the discussion. The representative of any community whatsoever can interrupt the value discussion as follows: "You have not convinced us, but we want to *give* you something: it will therefore take place according to your values."

The circumstance that in a given action one decides for this or that leading value places people in a *dilemma: the dilemma of morqlity*. The dilemma of morality involves the fact that in our action we cannot observe all the norms which we recognise to be universally valid. Hence the action cannot make any claim to universal validity, even though we simultaneously uphold the universal validity of these norms.

Therefore, when in an action it is necessary to choose between the three ideals, which ideal we choose *is a decision which we take on our own responsibility*. This responsibility is something which we cannot pass on to anyone else. One can say: "You have not convinced me, but in contradiction to the ideal of value discussion, I hereby decide to recognise and satisfy the other person's need. I know that my action cannot make any claim to universal validity; I cannot wish that everyone acted in the same way as me. In my action I have concretely weighed up the concrete situation and the concrete needs of the other person. Yet I vouch for the positive moral content of my action and take responsibility for it."

We have already seen that in the bourgeois world there are extraordinary obstacles to any conscious recognition and solution of the dilemma of morality; we have already seen how the dilemma of morality is replaced by a rationalisation of particularistic motives. Hence the bourgeois world epoch cannot have any immanent ethic of substantive values: the immanent ethic of values becomes formal.

The dilemma of morality has to be formulated, interpreted and consciously represented on the basis of a substantive ethic of values. Therefore, if we put forward a proposal for the conscious acceptance of this dilemma, in a particular context and up to a particular point, we have to have recourse to the substantive ethic of values. We have therefore conceived our radical utopia so that it is guided *by three substantive value ideas* on which an initial consensus exists. At the same time however, we find the purely substantive ethic of values *incompatible* with particular formulations of the value idea of freedom, formulations which as true values must not be excluded from this same rational utopia. What is involved here is the freedom to choose values and the plurality of forms of life in relation both to individuals and to communities. For this reason we propose *a "combination" of substantive and formal ethics of values.* That is to say, a combination which conceives everyone as having the capacity to presuppose the universal validity of value ideas, to act autonomously and to accept personal responsibility for all acts of value choice and for all value rational action.

Value rational action has two "stages". First, one has to choose the values and in every concrete individual case decide which norms ought to be observed, given the particular circumstances, aim and people involved; then one has to decide which values should have priority. The dilemma of morality can manifest itself in this decision, but it does not necessarily do so. After all, situations do occur in which not all the values can be observed, because the situation itself involves a conflict of values; there are other situations in which it is *unnecessary* to observe all the values, since those that are adequate to the situation, the person and the circumstances are enough.

The substantive value ethic has the following structure: *it presupposes a consensus in society at least in relation to the most general value ideas*; it demands of everyone that they compare their actions with these value ideas and that they relate their actions to them. At the same time, the concrete realisation of the values is left up to the *individual*, and *no* binding norm at all is laid down as to *how* they are to be observed. This presupposes a homogeneity of value ideas, at least to the extent that *they must not contradict each other*. For example, Aristotle's value ideas — wisdom, courage, justice, moderation, happiness (to name only the most important) — do not contradict each other in any way, and on all of them there existed a social consensus.

With one — from our point of view essential — difference,

we ascribe a similar structure to the value ethic which suits "chosen" communities of free people. For us our radical utopia involves a plurality of forms of life. Hence we are not positing a single homogeneous community, but rather a multitude of differing communities which vary amongst each other in terms of their systems of needs and their affinity to the corresponding values. In this context, a "chosen community" means that every person can freely choose to which community they want to belong and to which they do not. In other words, they can select values with a particular affinity to particular systems of needs which they promise to observe in their own form of life. In no way therefore do we want to eliminate from our radical utopia the *achievement of bourgeois society*, an achievement which in Athens was still unknown — namely value choice. Hence in place of the Aristotelian substantive value ethic with its two "stages" we propose a structure with *three stages*, in which *the second stage contains a formal criterion*: we link the substantive value ethic with the formal value ethic.

The first stage is the consensus on the nature of the three leading values as the *unconditional reference system* of all actions with a moral content. The second stage is the choice of those values which, as *true values*, can be brought into relationship with a leading value without contradiction and which guide value rational action — they are continuously upheld and are recognised by at least one community. The third stage is formed by the *realisation* of these values in action. Value choice, like action, takes place on the responsibility of the individual personality: *no* social norm *of any sort*, *no concrete duty* and *no concrete norm* functions as an unconditional imperative.

The observance of the norm of philosophical value discussion therefore presupposes the following formula: "Argue reasonably when it is your duty to do so — whenever, wherever, in relation to whatever question and in relation to whatever person you ought to!"

The norm which enjoins us to recognise and satisfy the needs of others can be observed in concrete action through the formula: "Recognise the needs of others when it is your duty to do so, and satisfy them how, when, where, in relation to whomever and whatever it is your duty to do so." In relation to the recognition of needs, "when it is your duty to do so" means nothing other than that in every situation and at every time one has to assess whether the need that raises the claim to recognition does not in fact include using other people as a mere means.

As an ultimate value, the multi-faceted development of abilities and needs through the appropriation of the wealth of society presupposes in concrete action the following formula: "Contribute to the development of the wealth of society how, when, and in whatever context it is your duty to do so; develop your abilities how and where you ought to, develop them in whatever context, in relation to whomever or whatever and for whatever purpose you ought to."

The formulas which have been put forward in relation to value ideas clearly also apply to the application of all chosen and true values. It is people themselves who have to decide whether in a particular situation and concerning a particular person *they* will react with an active offer of, for example, love, understanding or self-sacrifice; whether in a value discussion they will prioritise justice or mercy; whether from the tasks open to them they will select those which develop their will-power or those that develop their concrete talents, etc. Each individual personality always has to decide for themselves and on their own responsibility how values are to be applied in ways that are adequate to the subject and to the situation. The concept of adequacy to the subject involves both adequacy to the acting subject and adequacy to the subject whom the action affects. The moral personality is formed and perfected by making good decisions (and by revoking after the event false and bad decisions), and by consciously accepting responsibility for them.

A value ethic which is conceptualised in this way retains the imperative character of the good. Indeed, all values and actions *ought* to be related to the three ideas of value. If other systems of social rules conflict with one of the ideals of value, then it is people's *duty* to decide in favour of this value idea and its observance. The same ideas are also the criterion for judging the moral content of a deed. If a person's values conflict with these ideals, then that person is to be characterised as bad or evil; if someone chooses usefulness or success in *contradiction* to the ideas and not in agreement with them, then their deeds will be disapproved of.

At the same time, a value ethic which is conceptualised in this way goes *beyond duty*, for it does not lay down *a single concrete act* as duty. It is no longer possible for any social norm whatsoever to lay down what has to be done in this or that concrete case: the decision is left up to the individual. Ethics ceases to be a structure of concrete systems of rules and a system of differing or even mutually contradictory demands (as is the case with the morality of strata or classes, of religion, of the public and private spheres, of business, politics and sexuality, etc.), where the confusion of concrete rules expresses the variety of normative standards. In the value ethic that we are proposing, the ego is no longer caught in the crossfire of particularistic motivations and heteronomous normative systems. So long as morality remains a system of rules, then of necessity it will also have a heteronomous relationship to the individuality of the acting person; the binding character of its norms *will not only develop the individual personality, but will put restrictions on it as well. By contrast, the alienation of morality is abolished the moment the moral personality itself — the autonomous personality — becomes the carrier of the moral law,* and not merely as a rational being, *but as a whole person.*

However, it is only possible to imagine that individuals as moral personalities become the sole carriers of the moral law in an infinite process. The idea of this infinite process belongs to an ethics which goes beyond duty.

We have *not* posited our rational utopia as a world beyond duty. For us the starting point of this rational utopia is consensus on the three leading value ideas, and value ideas impose duties on us. At the same time morality can cease to be a system of rules: in their actions every human being has to apply the universal norms on their own responsibility, according to their own judgement, moral feeling and intelligence — the concrete web of duties no longer exists. We also include in our rational utopia an ethics in which the first and the second ethics of Lukács — the ethics of the "good" and of the "personality" — merge into a *single* ethics, an ethics in which continual progress means the continual reduction of the aspect of duty. Only in the world of such a morality can the autonomous moral personality develop, perfect itself, universalise itself.

THE PHILOSOPHY OF LEFT-WING RADICALISM

Up to this point we have been analysing the ideals which belong to the radical utopia: our analysis therefore has involved what ought to be. These ideals were generalised on the basis of the value judgements "Not this but that is true", "Not this but that is good" and "Not this but that is beautiful".

With the aid of these ideals, generalised from our value judgements, we have subjected what currently exists to a total critique. That is to say, *up to now* we have been following the usual path of "philosophy".

However, we know that philosophy is also capable of deducing its ought from what is. We have indeed seen that this deduction frequently involves an aspect of fruitful inconsequence. Yet the fact that the deduction occurs by means of a fruitful inconsequence is only clear to the recipient. Philosophers themselves strive to be consequential and are convinced that from alpha to omega their deduction corresponds to this criterion. If philosophers themselves *know* that what for them ought to be *cannot* be *deduced* from what is, then their philosophy as *philosophy* is incomplete.

I must confess that I *cannot philosophically deduce the ought of radical philosophy from what is.* Yet at the same time I am claiming that the ought of radical philosophy cannot in any way be deduced philosophically from existence within relationships of subordination and superordination. As soon as we relate our three ideals *as norms* to what is, then they all lead to *antinomies*.

The *first* antinomy has already been discussed extensively. Let us recall the two ways in which it can be formulated. Philosophical value discussion ought to be generalised; in a society based on relationships of subordination and superordination philosophical value discussion cannot be generalised, thus in a society based on relationships of subordination and superordination no philosophical value discussion is possible. To recall the earlier conclusion: the antinomy can be resolved in its second formulation, and through this resolution the first formulation too can *also be resolved*. This resolution however is only conceivable in *praxis*. This amounts to saying that philosophically the antinomy is unresolvable, and that from this point of view philosophy cannot *mediate between what is and what ought to be*.

Let us now glance at the second ideal. The norm "Every need must be recognised" applies exclusively to needs in which people do not serve as mere means for other people. It presupposes pluralistic systems of needs, which — bearing in mind social progress — do not mutually exclude each other. There must not be any need which for its satisfaction presupposes *in principle* that another need is unsatisfied. In brief: needs are not expressed through the mediation of interests.

However, relationships of subordination and superordination *necessarily* also involve needs in which people do serve as means for other people. In a society based on relationships of subordination and superordination needs are expressed as *interests*, and as conflicts of interest. Even radical needs — mostly — find their expression through the mediation of interests as conflicts of interests. Hence to demand that all interests ought to be recognised is *absurd*. Accepting one interest involves rejecting another.

It follows that the antinomy is that whereas all needs have to be recognised, in a society based on relationships of subordination and superordination all needs *cannot* and *must not* be recognised. All needs ought to be satisfied, yet in a society based on relationships of subordination and superordination they *cannot* all be satisfied. In such a society, even continual progress is only conceivable as the *progress of conflicts of interest*, and needs take alienated and quantitative forms (greed, ambition, lust for power), forms in which they are *limitless* and hence *insatiable*.

This antinomy too can be resolved, but once again only in *praxis*. It can be resolved by space being won for radical needs and radical structures of needs, by the step-by-step reduction of relationships and contradictons of interest in a total *social* revolution. Purely *philosophically* however, this antinomy cannot be abolished. Here too philosophy alone *cannot* mediate between what is and what ought to be.

And now briefly to the antinomy of the third ideal. Every person ought to develop their own abilities and needs by appropriating the wealth of society — yet in a society based on relationships of subordination and superordination every person *cannot* develop their own abilities and the needs which involve these abilities, *because* the society is one of a quasi-natural *division of labour* and of social inequality. This society produces personalities with one-sidedly developed abilities, personalities which are the result of people's places within the division of labour and the role expectations that go with them. This antinomy too can only be resolved in practice in the course of the abolition of the quasi-natural division of labour — in the course of total social revolution. Here too no philosophical mediation is possible between what is and what ought to be.

Yet does the idea of "total social revolution" fulfil the function of philosophical mediation? In our opinion it does *not*, and for the following reasons. The philosophical idea of total social revolution leads to a *vicious circle*, to a *circulus vitiosus*, to the problem of the chicken and the egg. Put simply: if people are to change, then the world has to change, but if the world is to change, then people have to change. Yet in philosophy no vicious circles are allowed.

There is only one thing that philosophy can do. It can give the world a norm, and it can will *people to want to give a world to the norm.* One has to assume that philosophy's norms accord with the needs of people, and this at least is something that philosophy can assume, for it has developed its norms in accordance with existing needs. And philosophy must know that the *idea* of total social revolution does not in any way mediate between what is and what ought to be, since it involves a vicious circle. Only total social revolution *itself* can mediate between what is and what ought to be, for concrete deeds (and indeed every individual concrete deed) dissolve in practice the vicious circle here and now. One can only repeat: philosophy, radical philosophy, has to become praxis, so that praxis becomes theoretical. *The philosopher mediates between what is and what ought to be, not as a philosopher but as a person*: as one person amongst millions, as *one* of those who want the world to be a home for humanity.

Notes

1 An Austrian economic and social historian (1886–1964) who lived for a long time in Budapest.
2 Wittgenstein's *Tractatus Logico-Philosophicus*.
3 Sub specie aeternitatis — from the viewpoint of eternity (Spinoza); écrasez l'infâme — destroy what is mean (Voltaire).
4 It is very probable that *every* objectification is poly-functional.
5 Wisdom very frequently also contains the beautiful, but for the moment we do not want to consider this aspect.
6 The claim that no one can find it, because it does not exist, is simply the reverse side of "finding".
7 *Hamlet* act II, scene 2.
8 Heller is here referring to a favourite expression of Kant's, the "architectonic" (editor's note).
9 Agora — citizens' assembly in ancient Greece.
10 Cf. note 3.
11 Equally, in philosophical reception a negative catharsis is possible. It follows the formula: "Now I know and now I see that everything is meaningless."
12 Malgré elle-même — despite itself.
13 Kant's conception of the regulatory practical idea is an example of such an insight.
14 Here we are considering the reception of philosophy as political ideology.
15 Weber understood himself to be a recipient of neo-Kantian philosophy, but this does not detract at all from the fact that everything in his work which is original philosophy he created himself.
16 In my book *Die Ethik des Aristoteles und das antike Ethos*.
17 Cf. note 3.
18 Hegel incidentally applies some categories which can only be related to philosophy. One of these is the concept of the concrete generality, and the claim that the whole is the true. If one considers his system in its entirety this is not surprising, for it is precisely in philosophy that the world spirit recognises itself.

19 The beautiful must here be excluded, for from Descartes to Kant it lies "beyond" the leading idea of philosophy.

20 I have attempted to discuss this in more detail in my book *Das Alltagsleben;* English translation, *Everyday Life*, forthcoming.

21 Kant XI. 129.

22 In relation to the economy Aristotle's stand point is not completely clear, and indeed it cannot be. He partly ascribes it to the category energeia and so understands it as value rational, but he partly ascribes it to the category techné — as for example the case of so-called "slave-holding" — and then describes it as purposive rational. The economy is doubtless the model for Max Weber's purposive rationality, and rightly so. To the extent that the economy made itself independent of the rest of society, so it *became* the characteristic sphere of purposive rationality in bourgeois society.

23 I have attempted to do this in my work *Theorie der Bedürfnisse bei Marx;* English translation, *The Theory of Need in Marx* (1976).

Index

196 INDEX

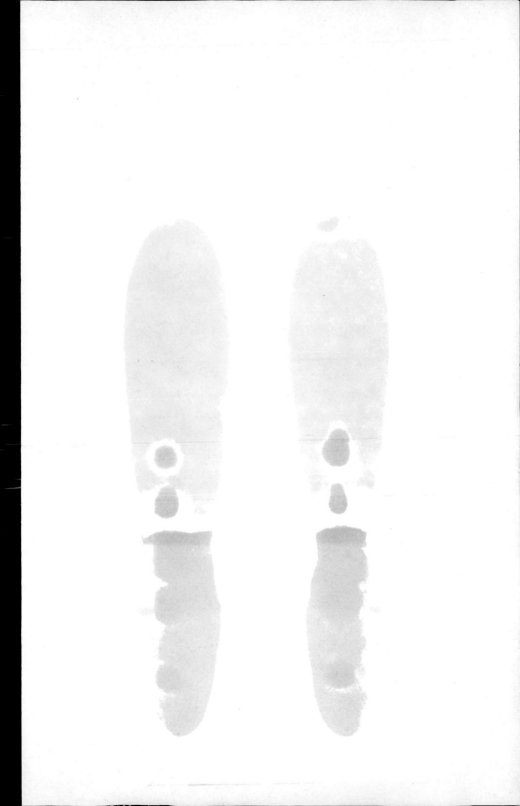